Thomas Ellwood

Landnama Book of Iceland as It illustrates the Dialect, Place Names, Folk Lore,

and Antiquities of Cumberland, Westmorland, and North Lancashire.

Thomas Ellwood

Landnama Book of Iceland as It illustrates the Dialect, Place Names, Folk Lore, *and Antiquities of Cumberland, Westmorland, and North Lancashire.*

ISBN/EAN: 9783337319663

Printed in Europe, USA, Canada, Australia, Japan

Cover: Foto ©Andreas Hilbeck / pixelio.de

More available books at **www.hansebooks.com**

THE

LANDNAMA BOOK OF ICELAND

AS IT ILLUSTRATES THE

DIALECT, PLACE NAMES, FOLK LORE, & ANTIQUITIES
OF CUMBERLAND, WESTMORLAND, AND
NORTH LANCASHIRE.

———

BY REV. T. ELLWOOD, M.A.,

RECTOR OF TORVER.

———

KENDAL:
T. WILSON, PRINTER, 28, HIGHGATE.
—
1894.

WORKS AND AUTHORS REFERRED TO.

First I have tried to trace out the very close connexion between the early Norse settlers in the North of Britain and Iceland, their Language, Place Names, and Folklore, from a careful reading and rendering of the Landnama itself, and on this I have based the Introduction.

I have also obtained much help in Words and Early History from the Icelandic English Dictionary of Cleasby and Vigfusson ; also Sturlunga Saga (two vols.), Corpus Poeticum Boreale (2 vols.), all from Clarendon Press ; also Saga Library, in several vols. (Morris and Magnusson) ; Northmen in Cumberland and Westmorland (Ferguson).

" A Bran Naw Wark," published at Kendal, in 1785, with a second title " A Plain Address written in the provincial dialect of the Barony of Kendal," by Rev. W. Hutton, Rector of Beetham from 1762 until 1811, I have found useful in looking out some of the older words and phrases of the Old Westmorland Dialect. This work was edited by the Rev. Professor Skeat, and published by English Dialect Society in 1879. It contains a Glossary with about 320 dialect words, and this as far I know is the only printed Glossary of the Westmorland Dialect as distinct from those of Cumberland and North Lancashire. To Professor Skeat, who presented me with this volume some years ago, I here make my grateful acknowledgments.

I have also referred to the kind help received from Mr. Magnusson in the passages where I have quoted that help, and I here acknowledge the most cordial manner in which that help has been given.

CONTENTS.

Introduction—Including a Description of the Physical Charac-
teristics of Iceland and a brief sketch of its first Settlement
by the Norsemen.

IN the year 1869, and for one or two years following,
Dr. Kitchin, now Dean of Winchester, took up his
abode at Brantwood, near to this parish and on the opposite margin of the Lake of Coniston, and while there he
had in hand as delegate of the Clarendon Press, Oxford, the
proofs of Cleasby and Vigfusson's Icelandic Dictionary,
which was then passing through the press.

Knowing that I was a Cumbrian, he kindly asked me to
look over these proofs and see whether I could suggest
affinities to our Cumberland, Westmorland, and Furness
Dialect. I was able to point out a number of words which
were identical or nearly so in the Icelandic and the dialect
of Cumberland and this portion of Lakeland, but as a
considerable portion of the work had passed through the
press it was too late for many of the dialect words I have
noted to appear in the work. In looking over the proofs,
however, and reading the exhaustive introduction to the
joint labours of Cleasby and Vigfusson, those long and
self-sacrificing labours in which Cleasby spent and finished
his life, light seemed to be thrown upon our northern
language and customs, which placed them in a point of
view very different from anything I had ever thought of
before.

The language of the Northmen had at the time of the
Settlement, been carried to Iceland, and there, isolated
and remote from the contact of other languages, it had in
a great measure preserved its primitive grammar and
vocabulary, so that the Icelandic Classics of a thousand
years ago, could with little difficulty be read by the Icelandic

landic peasant of the present day. It occupied, moreover, much the same relationship to the Danish and the other Norse tongues, that Latin does to the Romance language of Europe and hence its vocabulary was the best means of acquiring a radical knowledge of them.

It occured to me that the task of collecting such words of the dialect of Cumberland, Westmorland, and Furness as seemed to have identity or close affinity in form and usage with the Icelandic would be the best means of tracing out the origin of this dialect, and hence in some measure the origin of those by whom this dialect was spoken, and as we have here words and usages almost as primitive as they have in Iceland, we could, I thought, trace the language a great way towards its primitive or parent stock.

It occured to me also that as many of the old customs and superstitions in Lakeland are fast dying out, just as the old Norse words that represent them have become or are rapidly becoming obsolete, it must be now or never with me in commencing the undertaking, if I wished permanently to note down the customs and vocables of the people amongst whom the whole of my life has been spent.

I have worked at intervals at the task of collecting these words for a period of now nearly 25 years, and though I have doubtless in some instances done over again what others have done much better before me, yet in other instances I imagine I have unearthed and identified words and customs of the Northmen yet to be found amongst our dalesmen of which not any notice had been taken before.

Dr. A. J. Ellis,* in his exhaustive work upon the Dialects of Britain, has shown that there are several varieties

---

* In his fifth volume of " Existing Dialects, as compared with early English Pronunciation," Dr. Ellis gives fifteen varieties of the Cumberland Dialect, ten of the Westmorland, and seven of the dialects of Furness and Cartmel. These perhaps can hardly with strictness be called varieties. There are, however, differences in every case, though mostly only phonetic.

of

of dialect in the district of which I am treating, which includes the whole of Cumberland, Westmorland, High and Low Furness and Cartmel, and is thus in some measure conterminous with the Carlisle Diocese.

But the varieties of which he treats are purely phonetic in their character, and do not include any radical or derivative differences, and if you find one undoubted Norse word in the dialect of any portion of that area of which I have spoken the chances are that it has survived in every other rural portion of that district provided that portion has an " oldest inhabitant " with years long enough and memory keen enough to retain the customs and vocables of sixty or seventy years ago. I refer to Dr. Ellis in this connexion with great pleasure. I corresponded with him on the subject of the Cumberland and Furness dialect from 1872 close up to the time of his death ; at times, for weeks, numerous and voluminous letters passed between us on the subject; we were making up word lists however upon very different lines and from very different stand points, for he took the dialect in a purely phonetic while I took it so far as I could in a purely derivative aspect, but throughout this correspondence Dr. Ellis was always most willing to communicate anything I required from his extensive and unrivalled word lists and researches, and the last communication I received from him was a present of the concluding volume of his immense work upon the Dialects, and shortly afterwards, having completed in these volumes what may well be regarded as his life work, when his task was over he fell asleep.

It seems in many instances to be the opinion of philologists who have treated upon our dialect, as derived from the Norsemen, that as they were plunderers, so all our names and habits of plundering must in a great measure be referred to them. A careful study however of the Norse words in these dialects has led me to a very different conclusion. The remarkable thing about those

words

words is that they evince the peaceful disposition of those
Norsemen who first settled here and left their customs
and language. The great bulk of the words are field *
names and farm names, the terms applied to husbandry
operations, and names applied in the keeping and rearing
of sheep and cattle or used in their cure and management,
words applied to butter making, cheese making, knitting,
and all the domestic duties and concerns of everyday life.

Another consideration that adds interest to this study is
that the words correspond in the two languages not only
in their original idea and meaning, but in most of the
secondary and consequent meanings that are derived from
them and show that we have in Lakeland retained not
only many of the original vocables, but also the habits,
the customs and the superstitions, the folklore and the
modes of life which are common to the nations of the
northern stock. In pursuing this study it has been of
immense service to me that I have never lived outside the
district in which these Norse words, habits, and fashions
are still retained, and that I have lived generally in the
most rural, isolated and consequently unchanged portions
of it, that my inquiries, my word lists, and my everyday
life have been formed amongst a people where the earliest
words and customs are still retained if they are retained
anywhere, and that I have had leisure to read through,
more than once, for the purposes of comparison with the
dialect, the whole of the stupendous work of Cleasby and
Vigfusson, taking it throughout page by page and word by
word.

Whoever has read the life of Cleasby and the account
which it gives of his efforts to obtain a full knowledge of
all that was concerned in the elucidation of the early
language of the Norsemen, must remember how perti-
naceously he went time after time to Upsala to consult

---

* See Glossary of Norse Fell, Field and Farm names at the end of this volume.

and collate the Moeso-Gothic Bible of Ulphilas, of which the most valuable copy (the Argentine) is contained in the University Library of that place. There is a very close correspondence between this and the Icelandic. I have found also remarkable affinities between our northern dialects and this, the only remnant of the Language and Literature of the Moeso-Goths. Who was Ulphilas? He was a Bishop of the Moeso-Goths, and lived between A.D. 311 and 381. His version of the Bible, which was made about A.D. 370. is also valuable as a critical evidence to the New Testament. By it he contrived both to fix the Gothic language and to perpetuate Christianity amongst the Gothic people.

All that now remain of this version are fragments of the Four Gospels—about forty verses of Epistle to Romans, also portions of the other Epistles of St. Paul, and very small and fragmentary portions of certain books of the Old Testament. The term Moeso in Moeso-Gothic is taken to denote the language of the Visigoths who at one time dwelt in Moesia. The Visigoths are the West Goths as distinguished from the Ostrogoths or East Goths.

Some of the older words in our Northern Dialect seem to be identical both in sound and meaning with the words found in the existing fragments of Ulphilas. I have carefully collated what remains of Ulphilas with the words to be found in our dialect, and I think I shall be able to subjoin evidence that we have words in everyday use in Cumberland and here in High Furness, identical both in form and meaning with the words used by Ulphilas in his translation fifteen hundred years ago.*

* In John X., 1 verse,, Gard is used of the sheep fold,—a place enclosed for their protection. In Cumberland we have Gards of the enclosed fields; it is also used of land near Coniston. The Icelandic form of the word is Garth, which we have very commonly of the *enclosed* field near a house. In place-names in this form it occurs most abundantly in Lakeland. In the same chapter of St. John, the Shepherd is called Hairdeis (from Hairda,—a herd or flock), and the keeper of sheep and cattle upon the Cumberland marshes is still always called The Hurd. The moudiwarp is a Cumberland and Furness name for the mole and in

And

And this is the more remarkable, as Ulphilas had to reduce in some measure a spoken to a written language, and had himself to frame the characters by which he represented the words.

These fragments of the Moeso-Gothic have a remarkable resemblance to early English, but the resemblance, as will be seen in the passages I have given, is most especially marked in those early English words that still linger on in our Northern Dialects, and it is in these words that we can trace out how clearly the Moeso-Gothic and our own dialect are both allied to the Norse.

The Moeso-Gothic and the Icelandic have each as it were stereotyped a language and preserved its original grammar and vocabulary including its inflections which are so very different from anything that is used in modern language.

In Moeso-Gothic there is preserved in a Bible Translation the language of 1500 years ago, and in the Icelandic is preserved—if not the same language as the Moeso-Gothic at anyrate a twin brother of that language—corresponding most evidently in words, in inflexion and in origin, stereotyped and perpetuated through a long line of legends, sagas, and other historical records for more than a thousand years.

---

the Moeso Gothic Bible *Molda* is earth and *Wairpan* to cast up, and surely there could be no more appropriate name for the mole than "the caster up of earth or mould."

In Furness a farmer is said to smit or smear his sheep, and his peculiar smeared mark is called his smit—we have the same word smeitan in Ulphilas for smear or anoint. There is a remarkable correspondence in Ulphilas between the Icelandic and our northern dialect in the custom of reckoning years as winters. In three instances in the Bible of Ulphilas years are called winters. At Luke II., 42, Matthew IX., 20, and at Luke VIII., 42, namely in giving the age of Christ Himself, in describing how long the woman had the issue of blood, and in giving the age of the daughter of Jairus. In the Landnama years are also frequently called winters, notably in that passage which describes the first landing of Ingolf in Iceland as 6073 winters from the creation of the world. Vigfusson says that at present in Iceland peoples' ages are reckoned by winters instead of years. In this part of Lakeland a sheep of two years old is called a twinter,—that is, two winters, and a sheep of three years old is called a trinter,—that is, three winters, and Mr. Magnusson informs me that they have precisely the same terms for the age of sheep in Iceland.

And

And this language and its literature is the channel—I think almost the only channel through which have flowed to us—interesting old time records—not of Iceland alone but of all that concerned the early history, environments, and settlements of the whole of the northern race.

This is notably the case in the Heimskringla * or History of the Early Kings of Norway. It has an introduction containing a history of about thirty generations, of what are called Ynglings, who are the progenitors of the early Kings of Norway, and these Ynglings it derives from the race of Woden and the Gods. No doubt a good deal of the early portion of this history is mythical and legendary —yet not more mythical and legendary than other his‧ tories which profess to derive the early origin of Nations, and which, however authentic they may be for later times, generally set out from a region of fable and myth. In its later history the Heimskringla is always referred to as an authority, and its records are granted as the truth. And as the Icelanders have thus carefully preserved a record of external history, so they have been equally careful in the preservation of the history of their own island.

The very earliest record of the Settlement, and History of Iceland, is contained in the Landnáma Book.

This book, at once the Domesday and Golden Book of Iceland, is worthy to be ranked with the Bible of Ulphilas ; the Saxon Chronicle, and the Norman Survey, amongst foremost monuments of the history of our race. Opening with a brief sketch of the Settlement, it proceeds to give a notice of each settler (some 400 in all), his pedigree and descendants, and his claim in geographical order, beginning with the south firths and going completely round the island from west to east. This plan is filled in with a great mass of interesting detail, short accounts of famous

---

* Heims Kringla = *compass of the world,* and these are the two first words of the Introduction.

men

men and women, notices of old customs, laws, rites, and
nomenclature, verses and sayings, references to events
which took place abroad in England, Ireland, Scotland,
and the Eastern Scandinavian countries.

Arngrim who wrote in 1594, says of the early settlers,
that their names are recorded in those annals, together
with those of their numerous descendants, and also their
relations and their friends ; we are told therein what
coasts or inland territories they each of them settled and
occupied, and in what manner, and for what reason, the
first settlers gave names to the homesteads, nesses, hill-
ocks, brooks, rivers, dales, firths, creeks, mountains, and
islands, and how those early names are often retained,
and in use even to the present day. And this science of
the derivation of its early place-names, gives a peculiar
value to the Landnáma Book in a comparison with our
own country, for by the explanation thus given, the meaning and original application of existing place-names in
Iceland becomes very interesting, and throws a great
light upon our own local place-names, many of which
have evidently been given in the same language and by
the same race.

There is hardly anything more striking in the history
of the nations and languages of Europe, than that a
people numbering at various epochs of its history not
more than from 70,000 to 100,000 in all, should preserve
for over 1,000 years, its language intact, its literature,
rich, independent, and increasing in all its branches—and
its mythology certainly much the most perfect of any of
those that take Asgard for the abode of their divinities
and trace their origin to Woden and Thor.

The history of the preservation of this language in its
ancient form is remarkable.

The Icelandic language, called also the Norse and the
Danish, was spoken by the four great branches of the
Scandinavian race who people the countries bounding the
                                                    waters

waters of the Baltic—the Northmen—the Swedes—the Danes, and the Goths.*

At the beginning of the ninth century the growing population of these countries, together with political changes and the naturally enterprising character of the people, caused a great outward movement of the race. Under the guidance of their chieftains they set forth to seek for new homes in other lands, and thus the ninth century came to be known as the age of the Vikings. Two main currents of emigration by sea may be traced. First, the Danish, which directed its course to the north-east of England, and at length occupied that district so completely that it received the name of Dana-lagu.

The second migration was Norse. These settlers gradually peopled the coasts of Ireland, the Isle of Man, the shores of Morecambe Bay, and the western seaboard of Cumberland, the Orkneys and Shetland and the northern counties of Scotland, Ross, Moray, and especially Caithness. In the year 852 A.D., the Norse sea king Olave the White reached Ireland with a large fleet, and founded a Norse principality at Dublin. The foremost man amongst the Norsemen in Scotland and most closely, as we learn from the Landnama Book, concerned in its conquest was Sigard, the intimate friend of Thorsteinn, the son of King Olave the White.

Iceland seems to have formed the final and abiding limit of this stream of Norsemen. It had first been discovered by Naddod,† a Viking. He discovered no trace of population or any evidence of settlement. A deep snow fell upon the mountains while he remained there, so he called the country Snaeland or Snowland, which may remind us of Snaefell or Snowfell the name of the most

---

* The relationship of the Moeso-Gothic to the Icelandic and to our own dialect will thus be easy traced.

† Landnama, p. 26.

prominent

prominent mountain in the Isle of Man. The next discoverer as we have it in the Landnama Book was Gardar.* He sailed round it and so evidenced it to be an island. He spent one winter in the north, in Husavik or *housecreek*, evidently so called because he reared his temporary house there. He gave his name to the island and from him it was known as 'Gardarsholm. Thirdly, as we are told in the Landnama, it was visited by a noted Viking named Floki.† There is a curious sketch of his taking

---

* Landnama, p. 27.
† Landnama, p. 28.

The following description of the physical features of the island of Iceland will give an idea of the hardships encountered by the early discoverers and the original settlers :—

Iceland is an island in the most northern part of the Atlantic on the confines of the Arctic Ocean; in north latitude 63° 23′ to 66° 33′ and west longitude 13° 22′ to 24° 35′, distance about 600 miles from Norway, 250 from Greenland, 250 miles from the Faroe Islands, and about 500 miles from the north of Scotland. It belongs to the kingdom of Denmark. Its extent is about 39,207 square miles. Its extreme length from east to west is upwards of 300 miles, and its greatest breadth from north to south about 200 miles. Its coasts particularly on the north and west are very much broken by bays or fjords. It consists in part of lofty mountains, many of which are active volcanoes ; only certain level districts along the coast, and a few dales, are habitable or in any degree capable of cultivation, whilst even there scarcely a tree is to be seen. The interior of the island is almost entirely occupied by rugged traces of naked lava, and other volcanic products, vast icefields in many places connecting the high mountain summits, among which are prodigious glaciers in some instances descending even to the coasts, they and the torrents which gush from them, rendering communication between one inhabited spot and another, very difficult and dangerous. The highest mountain in the island is Ocrafa Jokul, which attains a height of 6,426 feet above the level of the sea. It is situated in the south east and is connected with a vast mountain mass, of which several of the summits are active volcanoes, no less than 3,000 square miles being perfectly covered with ice and snow at an elevation verging from 3,000 to 6,000 feet, whilst all underneath seems to be full of either active or smouldering volcanic fire. The most celebrated volcano is

three

three ravens with him that he might be directed by them in his approach in the Island. The first let loose flew around the mast, the second flew up into the air and so to and from the ship, the third flew from him without returning, and in following it he discovered the land.

He went up into a high mountain, and looking to the north over the fell he saw the Frith all filled with drift ice, and from this he called the country Iceland, which name it has ever since retained. Another word used by this northern Viking in his description of Iceland, as we have it in the Landnama, is of interest in connexion with our own dialect. He speaks of their temporary dwelling as Skalatoft, that is a shed used as a toft or dwelling. It will be seen from what I have said about those words elsewhere that we still retain them in the dialect in almost exactly their original meaning and form.

None of these, however, made more than a very transcient stay in the Island, the longest period hardly seems to have extended over a year.

Heckla. Krafla is perhaps the most noted of a great group of active volcanoes in the north of the island. The eruptions of Heckla have caused terrible destruction, while more terrible still have been those of Oerafa Jokul and others of the same volcanic mass. In repeated instances volcanic islets have been thrown up in the bays and near the coast of Iceland, which have generally disappeared again within a short time. Connected with the volcanic fires, are hot springs in great numbers, some of which flow gently, and others, called Geysirs, gush up at intervals and with ebullitions of great violence—numerous hot springs may in many places be seen sending up their steam in a single valley. The water of some is merely luke warm, whilst that of others is boiling; some are pure and some are sulphureous. They are subject to great variations, and appear and dry up very suddenly.

Earthquakes are frequent and the island suffered very severely from this cause in 1755 and in 1783. In the southern parts of Iceland the longest day lasts 20 hours and the shortest 4 hours. In the northern districts in summer the sun never sets for a whole week, and in winter never rises above the horizon for an equally long period of time.

The

The first settler was Ingolf the son of Orn, and his foster-brother Leif,* who set sail about 870, and reached Iceland ; they soon, however, passed on to Ireland, whence after a few years they returned to Iceland, taking with them a few Irish slaves. The date of this settlement seems to have been finally fixed as 874 A.D.

Leif had his name changed to Hjorleif on account of one of his exploits in Ireland, and in the description of his settlement in Iceland we have the use of two of what may be called test words of the identity between Icelandic and the dialect in the words he used for naming the house he built. It is said of him :—" Leif let þar gjora *skala* tva, ok er onnur *toftin* xviii faðma, en onnur xix," which means being translated :—"Leif caused them to make two scales or places of shelter, and one toft or dwelling was 18 fathoms and the other 19 in length." The definition of the skala, as given elsewhere, being that it was a square piece of ground with walls but without roof.

Leif† was drawn into an ambush and murdered by the colonists he had brought with him from Ireland, and then Ingolf remained, and so is regarded as the first settler in the Island.

About the same time Harald the Fairhaired had seized the throne of Norway, and by the establishment of despotic power had become unbearable to the high-spirited and independent chiefs, and therefore the Island, bleak and barren though it was, offered a welcome home to men who had hitherto lived in equal and undisputed rights. In the account of Harald the Fairhaired, as given in the Heimskringla or History of the Early Kings of Norway, by Snorri, it is said that a maiden called Gyda would consent to be his wife only on condition that he would subdue to himself the whole kingdom of Norway

* Landnama, p. 35.
† Landnama, p. 35.

and

and all its tribute and all rule over it. He accepted those conditions and made a solemn oath to the Gods that he would not cut his hair nor comb it until he had fulfilled his vow.

This process of subjugation went on for the next ten years, and had the effect of subduing many of the Norwegian chieftains, and of driving them with their scattered forces to Iceland.

Chapter xxiii. of his history, as given in the Heims-Kringla, describes the final accomplishment of his vow, and records that then his hair was combed and sheared for the first time of ten years after he had made his vow. While unkempt he had been called Shock Head, but now Earl Rognavold having combed and sheared him called him Harald Fairhaired, as all said he had most abundant and comely hair.

In connexion with this ten years war, the defeat at Hafursfirth seems to have been the most terrible discomfiture which Harald inflicted upon the recalcitrant Norwegian chieftains, and often, in the Landnama, it is said at the commencement of a settler's history that he came to Iceland from the defeat at Hafursfirth, having fled to Iceland doubtless because he was afraid to take refuge anywhere else.

Again, after the Norsemen in the British Isles had become unsettled by the death of King Thorsteinn the son of King Olave the White, in the year 874 A.D., they seem from that time to have begun to migrate to Iceland. The Landnama especially dwells upon the emigration of Queen Aud the widow of King Olave, who upon the death of her son, who was slain in battle, set forth for Iceland with almost all her kinsfolk and friends.

The number of those who sailed from the British Islands is probably about the same as that of those who had gone there from Norway. They carried with them their families, and such cultivation as they possessed. They

They spoke that form of the Scandinavian tongue which prevailed upon the western coast of Norway, whence they had originally come, and as time went on, while the new dialects formed themselves throughout Scandinavia, in Iceland the old tongue rose to the dignity of a literary language and thereby retained its old form. It has thus been preserved to our days.

The first settlers formed an independent aristocracy or republic which continued for nearly four hundred years. Up to the end of the tenth century, they held the heathen faith and practised the rites of heathen worship. Christianity was accepted as the faith of the island in the year 1000 A.D. In this respect, however, there must be a distinction made between the Norsemen who came directly from Norway or the east, and those Norsemen who having first settled in the British Islands are said to have come to Iceland from there or the west, or the western islands, by sea. It would seem from the following passage which I translate from page 321, that those last brought Christianity to Iceland with them but when they died there was a relapse to the old heathen faith. The passage is as follows * :—" So have wise men said that some of the settlers who come from the west by sea (er komu vestan um haf) and colonized Iceland had been baptized, these were named Helgi the Lean, and Orlygi and Helgi, and Jorundr the Christian, and Aud the Deep-eyed, and Ketil-Flatnose, and more men who came from the west by sea. Some of these retained Christanity to the day of their death, but that became extinguished in the course of generations so that some of their sons raised a heathen temple and sacrificed, and the land was altogether heathen for nearly one hundred otherwise one hundred and twenty winters."

I shall elsewhere give evidence that Queen Aud con-

* Landnama pp. 321 and 322.

tinued

tinued a Christian to the time of her death, yet the crosses that she had ordered to be reared at the place of her first settlement eventually became to her descendants objects of idolatrous veneration and worship. The place is called Kross holar on that account, and there are in the nomenclature of the island many other names with Kross prefixed to them which probably originated in the same way.*

The emigration by which the Norsemen sought Iceland from Britain seems to have been a gradual process of passing from island to island. They settled for a time, colonized and sometimes intermarried with the former settlers and then proceeded to go further north. The history of Queen Aud as given in the Landnama will give an illustration of what I mean, and it is probable from the distinguished position which she occupied amongst her countrymen, that she was the leader of a great many of them to Iceland and that they went by the same slow and gradual process by which she herself had gone. Upon the death of her husband she went to what, in the Landnama, are called the Sudreyjar† or Southern Islands, or Hebrides. There Thorsteinn her son married and there they seem to have staid for a considerable time.

In Scotland her son joined Sigurd in his conquest and they conquered more than half of Scotland, and over this Thorsteinn was made king. Like his father, however, he was slain in battle and Aud who had settled in Scotland

---

* Kross, Kross-a or Kross stream; Kross-dalr, Kross-ass, Kross-nes, Krossa-vik, Kross-vikingar, Kross-holt, Kross-holar, Kross-sund, and Krysi-vik in southern Iceland, probably from a harbour cross being erected. In this (the Carlisle) diocese there are at least seven parishes with names commencing in this way with cross, as Crosby-on-Eden, Crosby Garrett, Crosby Ravensworth, Cross Canonby, Crosscrake, Crosthwaite, Kendal, and Crosthwaite, Keswick. In Cumberland and Westmorland the Icelandic form Cross is used as distinguished from Krysi (cruci), the Anglo-Saxon form and by *thwaite* and *crake* forming the other portion of those words are undoubtedly Norse.

† We retain this word in the title of a Bishopric—Sodor and Man—Sodor being Sudrey, or South Islands, or Hebrides which together with Man formed a Norse Bishopric with a metropolitan at Nidaros, this Bishopric continued until the fourteenth century.

while

while her son was in power there, upon his death set out for the Orkney Islands where another of her descendants was given by her in marriage and where she seems for sometime to have continued in settlement. She then set off for Iceland carrying with her most of her relations and dependents, the knowledge of agriculture, and Christanity as her religious creed.

She held, however, first to the Faroe or sheep islands, about half way between Great Britain and Iceland, and she staid long enough apparently to found a colony,. and she gave in marriage Alofa, the daughter of her son Thorsteinn the Red. She then went on to Iceland and settled Broadfirth in the best portion of the new country.

And there she exercised a mighty influence over the future history of Iceland. From her and her connections seem to have descended all that was great, noble, or learned in its history, and she seems to have sent on to many a generation the telling example of a virtuous and a devoted life.

In connection with the history of Queen Aud, her relations, and her numerous descendants as found in the Landnama may be noted the use of some of the most characteristic words and institutions that are common to the north English and Icelandic stock.

She settled the Dale lands about the year 892, and apparently gave land and liberty to all the slaves she had brought with her, for there is a detailed account of their settlement as well.

The crosses she reared on her first arrival resulted afterwards in cross worship.

Her Arval Banquet, an account of which I have given elsewhere, is the most remarkable instance of the kind mentioned in the Landnama and abounds in words cognate forms of which in our Dialect have survived almost to the present in connection with such occasions. The How or Burial Mound erected near to where she was
interred

interred* seems by its name and institution to mark a close connection with something similar in the various countries where she had resided and which she had assisted in settling as she went on in her journey to the north.

The How† or burial mound was looked upon as a great mark of distinction and there is a verb derived from this noun How or Haugr having a like meaning as applied to describe the burial of the father and son of Thoralf at page 92 of the Landnama. The How or burial mound of the Norse Chieftains was considered by their descendants as a sort of entrance to Valhalla or the world of the departed, and as such they came there that they might *die into it*, that is as has been explained elsewhere, that they might reside within it after their death.

---

* Queen Aud's directions about her burial in the space between high and low watermark do not seem to have been carried out in their literal acceptation.

† The How is a note of honourable burial and marks perhaps as well as any place-name our close connection with the Norse. In the north of England How originally meant a grave mound, and Miss Powley in a "Plea for Old Names," says that How is still in use for grave mound in Cumberland and Westmorland. In his "Forty Years in a Moorland Parish," Atkinson gives many instances of Hows having been exhumed in the North Riding of Yorkshire, and bones having been found in them. At a place in Torver parish called Bull How Moss, cairns have been examined and human remains found underneath.

Edmoston says that Howie still means a tumulus-mound or knoll in the Shetland and Orkney Islands. The Hill of Howth, near Dublin, may be quoted as marking the vicinity of one of the early stations of the Norsemen. As a place name in Cumberland and Westmorland the word How is applied to a mound or knoll, many instances of which are given in the Glossary at the end of this volume. In some cases actual examination has shown them to be graves, presumably of Norsemen.

The Landnama Book of Iceland, as it Illustrates the Dialect, Place Names, Folklore, and Antiquities of Cumberland, Westmorland, and North Lancashire.

By the Rev. T. Ellwood, M.A., Rector of Torver, Coniston.

With Notes and Additions by Eiríkr Magnússon, M.A.

THE title of the "Landnáma Book," like many other names when closely considered, contains within itself an epitome of its own meaning. With regard to the first portion of it, the word "Land" means land in Iceland as in England, and "nám," *n.*, in gen. pl., "náma," from the strong verb *nema, to take,* means a taking possession of, or settlement; hence the "Landnáma Bók" is the book describing the taking possession of or settlement of land in Iceland by those heads of families of Norsemen who colonised the island.* As I shall show presently, by an extract, the first date of this settlement is in A.D. 874, when Ingolf, four years after he discovered Iceland, made his home at Ern's-knoll (Arnarhóll) on the eastern side of the small bay of Reykjavík, round which is clustered the present capital of Iceland. And as this process of settlement was going on, at any rate for the next sixty years,† you will see that it synchronises well with the period when those same Norsemen first began to make their settlements upon the British and more especially upon our northern coasts; and I think it well in the outset to lay some stress upon this very close connection between the

---

* "Landnám," and "nema land," are namely, acts of purely private character, no idea of State interest or public policy being implied.—E.M.

† "Sixty years." Ari the Learned, in Íslendingabók, ch. 3, says:—"Svá, hafa oc spakir menn sagt, at á lx vetra yrdi Island albyggt, .svá at eigi væri meirr sídan": So have also wise men said that in lx. winters was Iceland fully settled so that no further (settlement) there has been since.—E.M.

time

time of the Icelandic and the time of the early British-
Norse settlement, for it has an essential bearing upon the
conclusion which I think will be more or less brought out
in this paper, which is that the same stock of Norsemen,
having at the same time colonised those two countries,
have left in each the same language, the same place-
names, and the same customs; and that a wonderful coin-
cidence can still be made out between them even at this
distance of over one thousand years.

There are striking differences between the mode in
which the Norsemen colonised England and the mode
in which they colonised Iceland. In England they
had a continual warfare; in Iceland, as we learn from
the Landnáma Bók, they made at first a quiet and un-
resisted settlement, because in the one case they went
to a well settled, in the other to an absolutely vacant
territory; the one in short was a conquest, the other, as
the name implies, was a quiet taking possession of land.
And yet the Landnáma Bók shows sufficiently that it was
the same race, the same tribes, and sometimes even the
very same men that were doing both the one and the
other. In the Landnáma Bók we have the names of the
men most familiarly known in our early English history,
who seem in that unquiet spirit that marked the early
Norsemen to have gone first to Iceland, and then to
Scotland and the north of England, or else for a time to
have tried Scotland or the north of England and to have
gone to Iceland after all. In the Landnáma Bók we
have also a record of the discovery of America by the
Norsemen. It is there called Vineland and also Greater
Ireland, because the Norsemen drifted thither over the
ocean from Ireland, and thought the tongue of the people
reminded them of, or was identical with, Erse.

The Landnáma Bók itself bears the impress of two
different hands. It was originally written by Ari Frodi,
that is Ari the historian who lived between 1067 and
1148

1148, and who was both a historian and a learned divine, but it was worked into its present form by Sturla Thordarson, who was born 1214 and died 1284.* It contains a register of the name of every man that settled in Iceland, and in most instances a record of his descendants and where they went, and it contains also a register of every house—farm and tribe or family name. There are 4,588 men's names, and 1,949 place, farm, or tribe names, and I mention these last more especially, as it is from them that I have taken the names that I have used in comparing their place names with our own. I have made my translations from the Copenhagen edition of 1843, which is the last edition that has appeared, and the numbers I have given in reference denote the page in that edition from which my translation was made. *The Clarendon Press* announced an edition some time ago, but I judge from latest inquiries that it has not yet appeared. I give the translation of eight passages. Seven of these I have made myself, but in the second, and much the most difficult and important passage, I have had the very

---

* The history of the composition of the Landnáma Bók is briefly this :—
  1. *Ari Thorgilsson*, the Learned, wrote the history of the settlements of the South, West, and North Quarter.
  2. Kolskegg Asbiornson, the Learned, his contemporary, described the East Quarter. Cfr Landnáma Bók, p. 249 : Nù heifir Kolskeggr fyrir sagt hédan frá um landnám=" Now has Kolskegg dictated (the story) henceforth as to the settlements.
  3. The joint work of these two was again edited by
  (a) *Styrmir*, the "Learned," son of *Kari* (ob. 1245). This edition was again gone over and revised, and no doubt added to by
  (b) Sturla Thordson (1214-1284) ; which recensions (a & b)
  (c) Hauk Erlendsson re-edited, his edition, the "Hauksbók," forming one of the principal texts of the Landnáma Bók.—There is a special recension also based on a and b, the so-called "Melabok," the author of which is not known, though there is no doubt that he was a Sturlung ; if not Marcus Thordson of Melar himself, then his son or grandson.—A prior Brand Halldórsson the Learned, of the 12th century, is also mentioned, not exactly as a writer of Landnáma, but as author of the genealogies of the men of Broadfirth, "Briedfirdingakyn." He may be a possible primary contributor to the great work that bear's Aris' name. What the later editors of Landnámabók did add to it, did no doubt, chiefly consist in genealogical lore ; they brought the lines down to their own immediate predecessors.—E.M.

able

able help of Eric Magnússon, assistant librarian of the Cambridge University Library, a native Icelander, and a distinguished philologist in England as well as in Iceland, and moreover one of the kindest and most willing helpers that ever it has been my good fortune to meet.

Bound up with the Landnáma Bók, and forming a portion of it, is a chronological table of the chief events that happened in Iceland, together with the names of the speakers of the parliament of the commonwealth (lögsögumenn), and when and where they flourished; and commencing with the first settlement in 874. I have given the record of this table for a period of about 400 years. The first translation is from the portion that records the very first settlement in Iceland 874. The original occurs at page 33, chapter vi. of Landnáma Bók. It is as follows :—   '

"Sumar þat, er þeir Ingólfr fóru til at byggja Ísland hafði Haraldr hárfagri verit xii. ár konungr at Noregi; þá var liðit frá upphafi þessa heims vi. þúsundir vetra ok lxxiii. vetr, en frá holdgan drottins dccc. ok lxxiiii. ár. Þeir höfðu samflot, þar til er þeir sá Ísland; þá skildi með þeim þá er Ingólfr sá Ísland, skaut hann fyri borð öndugis súlum sínum til heilla; hann mælti svá fyrir, at hann skyldi þar byggja er súlurna kæmi á land.* Hann var enn þriðja vetr undir Ingolfsfelli fyrir vestan Ölfusá. Þau missari fundu þeir Vifill ok Karli öndvegissúlur hans við Arnarhvál fyri neþan heiði. Ingolfr fór um várit ofan um heiði; han tók sér bústað þar sem öndvegissúlur hans höfðu á land komit; hann bjó í Reykjarvík; þar eru enn öndvegissúlur þær í eldhúsi." This passage I have rendered as follows :—

"That summer, when Ingolf and his companions went to settle in Iceland, Harold the Fairhaired had been king of Norway for twelve

---

* I have here omitted the portion that refers to the fortunes of Ingolf's companions, and continued the narrative when it again alludes to himself.—T.E.

years. At that time had passed from the beginning of the world 6,073 winters, and from the Incarnation of our Lord 874 years. They sailed together until they sighted Iceland, then they separated. When Ingolf saw Iceland he threw overboard his high-seat posts for good luck (or as an omen), and took a solemn oath that he would there build, where the high-seat posts should come upon shore. He passed the third winter at the foot of Ingolfsfell (a mountain named from him), on the west of Olfuswater. This year (his men) Vifill and Karli found his high seat posts near the *Ern-knoll* (Arnarhvál), beneath' the heath. * Ingolf went in that spring down across this heath, and he took up his abode where his seat posts had come to land. He dwelt at Reykjarvik, and his high-seat posts are still in the eldhouse "—literally fire-house (fire-hall).

I have quoted this passage at the outset, as it fixes with a sufficient degree of exactness the date of the first settlement of Iceland, namely, as given in this text 874 (less correctly given in the list of dates at the end of the Landnáma Bók as 875).

The most remarkable description in this and the following passage is the mode which those Norsemen took to guide them in the selection of their future home. The word I have translated high-seat posts is *öndugis súlur*,† and referred to the two pillars of the high-seat of the

---

* "Beneath the heath." You have here to deal with a very peculiar phrase of topography. The upland plateau which in a south-westerly direction runs down from the extinct volcano of Skjaldbreid, which lies far inland N.E. of Reykjavík, and terminates in the promontory of Reykjaness, is, for that portion which divides the lowlands of the Reykjavik region from those south and south-west of Ingolfsfell, called Mossfell's Heath, shortened generally in the sagas into Heath simply. Now all localities which lie in the *western* watershed of this heath are said to be "beneath," or "below," the Heath, while those *east* of it are said to be above the heath. This peculiar topographical expression must have arisen originally in the household of Ingolf at Reykjavik, or at Erno Knoll, while he, and his were under the impression that all localities east of the heath, being *inland* localities from the point of view of Ernknoll, were necessarily at a higher level above the sea than Reykjavik and its seaboard surroundings. We may, therefore, safely date this phrase as first originating in 874.—E.M.

† "Öndugis súlur" öndugis gen. of öndugi, n., contracted from önd-vegi, which is the common form. The derivation of the word is not quite settled yet. But the most probable derivation is from önd=porch, doorway, and vegr way. Öndvegis sæti is probably the original expression : the seat that faced the way along which arrivals to the hall made their progress up to the chief's presence. It is a noteworthy fact that no pillars or high-seat posts are mentioned dedicated to any other god but Thor. In the main the pillars were emblems of tribal chieftainship in its two principal aspects : martial leadership and priestly authority.—E.M.

father

father of the family, or chief, or priest, for they were all included in the same person. These were ornamented with carved figures of Thor ; hence you will find in the next passage it is called a Thor, and the place where it came ashore is called Thorness, just as Thursby, in Cumberland, is literally the dwelling of Thor. These seats then, or seat pillars, they brought with them when they sought new homes, and when near Iceland cast them overboard into the sea and let them drift ashore in whatever direction the tide took them ; and wherever they found them cast ashore there they built their home and formed their settlement, as the place marked out for them by the god. The high-seat, or chair so named, with its ornamented or carved posts, was looked upon as a symbol of the father's authority as a priest or a parent, and there is a record that the son was not allowed to sit in his father's seat until he had avenged his death. The curious way in which those chairs, or seat-posts, were carved and ornamented with figures was a very marked characteristic of them, and the very curious carved arm-chairs and high-backed chairs, yet to be found in old country houses in this neighbourhood, and highly prized and much sought after by collectors of carved work, may have had their origin from these ornamentally carved chairs, which were such an essential element in marking out the original homes of the Norsemen.

This passage is interesting in another point, for Reykja-vik,* of which it records the settlement, is, though but a village of somewhat about 4000 inhabitants, the present capital of the island.   It is literally reek town, or smoke

---

* The meaning of the name is Reek-wick ; wick meaning bay, or bight—not the wick which descends from Lat. vicus, hamlet, township. The name arises from the fact that in the close neighbourhood there are warm, steaming springs. —Do you mean Reykjaor Reyk-holt by Reck wood ? If so, the word "holt" in Iceland does not mean wood (holz) but a hill-rise, bare and exposed; perhaps Reek-Knoll would come near enough.—E.M.

town, reminding us of Auld Reekie, or Edinburgh of Burns. We all know what reek is in Cumberland, and reek as a place name occurs abundantly in Iceland ; there is Reek River, Reek Dale, Reek Ness, and Reek Wood, Reek Hole, and Reek Strand. We have the word most familiar in the dialect, but as a place-name it seems to be almost peculiar to Iceland. The pillars of transparent steam from the hot springs and geysers, as seen afar off, must have struck the minds of the first settlers, who gave names to the localities.

The word *eldhús*, or fire-house, used in this passage to describe the room where the high-seat was kept with superstitious reverence, is, I think, interesting, as the word *eld* for fire is a word that may be taken as a test of Scandinavian races as distinguished from the Teutonic, who use *feuer*—fire—which is wanting in Scandinavian.* We have *elding* for fuel all over Furness at any rate ; in fact, in High Furness, it seems until lately almost the only word thus used ; here then we have a very marked and close relationship.

The superstition of keeping up a sacred fire, as this passage seems to indicate, was by no means peculiar to Iceland ; the fire tended by the vestal virgins is sufficiently recorded, and one marked command about the Jewish Tabernacle was that *the fire shall not go out* ; the word "couvre feu," from which "curfew" is derived, would appear to mean to cover, or rake, and not altogether extinguish the fire. The fire was raked or covered in Iceland, and thus kept up from day to day continually, and anyone who is conversant—as I have been almost all my life—with our own portion of Lakeland, knows with

---

* Feuer, Engl. fire, does exist in Scandinavian, but only in technical usages ; and in Icelandic it only occurs in the ancient poets in the form of fúrr, fyrr. By-the-way, does "elding" ever occur in Cumberland in the sense of lightning? You know the word means fuel in Icelandic as well as in Cumberland, so the relationship is not only close, but identical.—E.M.

what

what superstitious reverence the old hearth fire was raked
or put in a condition of smouldering at nights, and so kept
up from day to day, from month to month, from year to
year, and from generation to generation, and, I certainly
knew, in more instances than one, homes where the fire
had been kept up for three generations; and during all
that time had been so zealously guarded that it had not
been once allowed to go out. There is a well-known instance in our own neighbourhood where a man had what
he called " his grandfather's fire ;" that is a fire that was
known to have been kept up without extinction for at
least three generations, that when it once accidentally
went out he went to some woodcutters who had lighted
their fire from his, and brought back from their fire a fire
to his own hearth, that thus he might preserve, as it
were, the seeds of his ancestors' original fire.

The next passage which I have, with the assistance of
Mr. Magnusson, translated from the Landnáma Bók,
refers to the settlement of Thorolf, and the establishment
of the Things, or local Legislative Assemblies, and I have
quoted it in connection with the first passage, as the date
of the first passage will enable us to fix the date of the
second with a tolerable degree of exactness, for Ingolf,
who is mentioned in the first, and Thorold, who is mentioned in the second, both left Norway for Iceland in the
reign of the same King (Harold the Fairhaired), and they
seem both to have been driven away by the unbearable
tyranny of his government, and they both went forth trust-
ing in the auspices of Thor as the guardian deity who
should guide them in safety to their future home. The
passage I now quote respecting Thorold is chap. 12 in the
second part of the Landnama Book, and it commences at
p. 96. I have translated it without any omission to the
end ; it is as follows :—12 Þórólfr, son Örnólfs fiskreka,
bjo í Mostr, því var hann kallaðr Mostrarskegg ; hann
var blótmaðr mikill, ok trúdi á Þór ; hann fór fyrir ofríki
Haralds

Haralds konúngs hárfagra til Íslands, ok sigldi fyrir
sunnan land ; en er hann kom vestr fyrir Breiðafjörd, þá
skaut hann fyrir borð öndvegis súlum sínum ; þar var
skorinn a þórr ; hann mælti svá fyrir, at þórr skyldi þar á
land koma, sem hann vildi at þórólfr bygði, hét hann
því, at helga þór allt landnám sitt, ok kenna við hann.
þórólfr sigldi inn á fjörðinn, ok gaf nafn firðinum, ok
kallaði Breiðafjörð ; hann tók land fyrir sunnan fjörðinn,
nær miðjum firðinum, þar fann hann þór rekinn í nesi einu;
þat heitir nú þórsnes. þeir lendu þar inn frá í váginn, er
þórólfr kàllaði Hofsvág ; þar reisti hann bæ sinn, okgjörði
þar hof mikit, ok hegalði þór, þar heita nú Hofstaðir.
Fjörðrinn var þá bygðr lítt eðr ekki. þórólfr nam land frá
Stafá inn til þórsár, ok kallaði þat allt þórsnes, hann hafði
svá mikinn átrúnað á fjall þat, er stóð í nesinu, er hann
kallaði Helgafell, at þangat skyldi engi maþr óþveginn líta,
ok þar var svá mikil friðhelgi, at aungu skyldi granda í
fjallinu, hvárki fé né mönnum, nema sjálft gengi á braut ;
þat var trúa þeirra þórólfs frænda, at þeir dæi allir í fjallit.
þar á nesinu, sem þórr kom á land, hafði þórólfr dóma alla,
ok þar var sett héraðsþing með ráði allra sveitarmanna. En
er menn voru þar á þinginu, þá skyldi víst eigi hafa álfreka
á landi, ok var ætlat til þess sker þat, er Dritsker heitir,
þvíat þeir vildu eigi saurga svá helgan völl sem þar var.
En þá er þórólfr var dauðr, en þorsteinn, son hans, var
ungr, þá vildu þeir þorgrímr Kjallaksson ok Asgeirr, mágr
hans, eigi ganga í skerit örna sinna ; þat þoldu eigi þórsnes-
singar, er þeir vildu saurga svá helgan völl, því börðust
þeir þorsteinn þorskalratr ok þorgeirr Kengr við þá þor-
grím ok féllu þar nökkurir menn, en margir urðu sárir, áðr
þeir urðu skildir. þórdr gellir sætti þà ; ok með því at
hvárugir vildu láta af sínu máli, þá var völlrinn óheilagr
af heiptar blóði. þá var þat ráð tekit, at færa brutt þaðan
þingit, ok inn í nesit, þar sem nú er; var þar þá helgistaðr
mikill ok þar stendr enn þórs steinn, er þeir brutu þá menn
um, er þeir blótuðu, ok þar hjá er sá dómhringr, er menn
skyldu

skyldu til blóts dæma. Þar setti ok Þórðr gellir fjor-
ðungsþing með ráði allra fjórðungs manna.   Son Þórólfs
Mostrarskeggja var Hallsteinn Þorskafjarðargoði, faðir
Þorsteins surts ens spaka ; Ósk var móðir Þorsteins surts,
dóttir Þorsteins rauðs.   Annarr son Þórólfs var Þorsteinn
Þorskabítr, hann átti Þóru, dóttur Ólafs feilans, systur
Þérðar gellis, þeirra son var Þorgrímr, faðir Snora goða,
ok Börkr enn digri, faðir Sáms, er Ásgeirr vá.

"'Thorolf, son of Ornolf—'Fishdriver,'—dwelt in Most-isle. He
was called Mostbeard ; he was a great man of blood offerings, and
believed in Thor.

He emigrated to Iceland on account of the tyranny of Harold the
Fairhaired, and sailed by the southern part of the land ; but when
he was came west, off Broadfirth, he threw overboard the high-seat
posts, whereon Thor was carved. And he prayed thereover that Thorr
(as he called the pillars) should come to land where the god wished
him to settle, and he promised that he would dedicate all the land of
his settlement (*landnám sitt*) to Thor, and name it after him. Thorolf
then sailed into the frith, and gave a name to the frith and called it
Broadfrith. He took land on the south side, near the middle of the
frith. There he found Thor cast ashore, upon a point of land which
is now called Thorsness on that account. They landed further
up the ness in the bay which he called Temple Bay (*Hofsvág*).
There he reared his home, and there he built a large temple and
consecrated it to Thor, and now the place is called Temple Stead
(*Hofstaðir*). The frith had been very sparsly settled before this time,
or not at all. Thorolf *took* land (*nam* land) from Staffriver inwards to
Thorsriver, and called all that part Thorsness. He had so great a
reverence for that fell which stands on the ness, and which he called
Helgafell—Holy Fell,—that he enjoined that thither should no man
unwashen look; and there was so great place-hallowness (sanctuary)
that nothing should be destroyed on the mountain, neither cattle
nor people, unless it should go away of its own accord. That was
the belief of them, Thorolf and his kinsmen, that they should die
into the mountain.*   There on the ness, where Thorr (Thor's pillar,
the high-seat post carved with Thor's image) came aland, Thorolf
had all the docms (law courts), and there was set up the district-

* " Die into the mountain," *i.e.*, would dwell within the mountain after their
death.—E.M.

assembly (legislative) by the advice of all the men of the country-side (the dependents of Thorolf, who formed his temple parish, as it were, he being their temple priest). But while men were at the Thing, easements should surely not be had on land (it was strictly forbidden to men to go on nature's errands on the land),* and for that purpose was set apart that skerry (sea cliff) which is called Dirt Skerry, for that they should not defile such a holy field as was there. But then when Thorolf was dead, and Thorstein, his son, still young, then they Thorgrim Kiallakson and Asgeir, his son-in-law, would not go into the skerry on their errands. This the Thoressings would not stand, that they should wish to defile so holy a field, therefore fought they, Thorstein Codbiter and Thorgeir Staple, against those Thorgrim and Asgeir, there at the Thing about the skerry, and certain men fell there and more got wounded, or ever they could be parted. .Thord the Yeller appeased them, and whereas neither side would yield, the field having been already defiled with the blood of the deadly feud (heipt, implacable or mortal hostility), this counsel was taken, to remove away from there the Thing (assembly) and take it up into the ness, where it now is; was there then a place of great hallowedness (sanctity), and there stands still the stone of Thor, over which they broke those men whom they sacrificed, and thereby is that doomring where people should be doomed (condemned) to sacrifice.

There also Thord the Yeller placed the quarter parliament, with the counsel of all the men in the quarter.

The son of Thorolf (Mostbeard) was Hallsteinn, priest of the men of Codfirth, father of Thorstein the Black, a wise man; † Osk was the mother of Thorsteinn the Black, and daughter of Thorsteinn the Red.

Another son of Thorolf was Thorsteinn Codbiter. He had Thora to wife, the daughter ot Olaf Feilan,‡ sister of Thord the Yeller. Their son was Thorgrim, father of Snorri the Priest, and Bork the Big, father of Sam whom Asgeir slew."

I may remark here, with regard to what I have trans-lated as the quarter parliament (fjordungs thing), that the

---

* Alf-rek (elf-chase), that which by its impurity drives away the pure and tender guardian spirits of the soil.—E.M.

† He was called the Wise because he reformed the calendar of Iceland, c. A.D. 960. Cfr. Islendingabók, ch. iv.—E.M.

‡ Feilan is a nickname, a word of Celtic origin, and uncertain sense.—T.E.

whole

whole of Iceland was divided into four divisions called
North, South, East, and West Quarters, and these divisions exist up to the present time.* Each of these divisions had a *fjordungs thing*, or quarter parliament, and
each had also a *fjordungs domr*, or quarter court.†

It will been seen at once that a good deal of the meaning of this passage, of its place names, proper names, and
that which more especially directed those Norsemen to
their early settlements, turns upon their devotion to Thor.
The high-seat post, of which I have here translated the
fortunes, was a carved image of Thor, carved upon the
back of the high chair used in his temple: hence it is
called the Thor, and marked out the place where they
should land and settle. The place that Thor occupied in
Scandinavian mythology is well known; he was the god of
thunder, the keeper of the hammer, the ever fighting slayer
of trolls and the queller and destroyer of all evil spirits, the
defender of the earth and the friend of mankind. There
are giants ready to assail the earth and its inhabitants in
the Scandinavian as in the classical mythology. Thor,
like Jupiter, meets them in a hard fought conflict, and some
of the finest lays and legends of the Edda, like the sublime
Metamorphoses of Ovid, are devoted to describing those
battles of the gods. It is Thor and his hammer who go
number one in these conflicts, and he and his attendant
divinities are always sketched as driving off those giants
as those malign and opposing influences who would destroy
and overturn the earth. Jack the Giant Killer, Tom Raw-
head and much of our northern nursery lore may have had

---

* The Quarter Division does exist no more for any administrative purpose. It
merely exists as a remembered item of antiquity, and a convenient geographical
expression.—E.M.

† You had better make it clear, that the institution of the Quarter Courts, by
Thord Yeller at the Althing in 964, had no connection with this fight between the
men of Thorness and the followers of Kiallak the Old. This feud raged A.D.
932-34. The Quarter thing here spoken of was the rural court, or first instance,
before which cases out of the quarter could come. The Quarter Courts at the
Althing were of a quite different constitution.—E.M.

its origin from Thor and his conflicts. The stones and cairns, like the law mounds and doomcircles, were consecrated to him, and Vigfusson quotes this inscription from a heathen Danish Runic stone : "þurr vigi þassi runar." —" Thor consecrate these runes." We certainly have evidence of such a worship and such an influence in some of our northern names. Thursday marks this, and I think it is very likely that the name was first so applied in the northern portion of England, for yet those who speak in the dialect do not call it Thursday but Thorsday. The derivation of the place-name Thursby is very directly shown in the passage I have just translated. Thur is no doubt, I think, Thor ; and by=bae, which in the Icelandic means a homestead or dwelling, and this bae is the very word in the original Icelandic for homestead in that passage which I have translated.* " There he raised his homestead, and there he built a large temple, and consecrated to Thor the place." Runic and other stones dedicated to the divinity were called Thor's stones or Thorsteinn ; hence by an obvious transition became place-names or personal names. We have an evidence of this in more than one instance in the north. You have Thurstonfield near Carlisle, and the old name of Coniston Lake in High Furness was Thurston, or Thurstone Water, and the name is still preserved in Thurston Ville, a residence at a short distance from the foot of the Lake.

There is one place in this passage which, from the institution connected with it, is of very considerable importance, and that is the word dómhringr—Doomcircle— the doom ring or judgment ring. The courts of the heathen Norsemen were surrounded by this domhringr, about a bowshot from the centre where the benches were placed ; and no evildoer might enter this ring, or commit

---

* The declension of bær :—Bær, bæ, by,—a dwelling.

an act of violence within it; if he did so he was called a *vargr í veum*—"a wolf in the holy place." We have the date of the institution of those quarter courts, one for each of the four political divisions of the county, as they are here instituted by Thord the Yeller, namely, in the year 964; and at a later date a Fifth High Court, called Fimtar-dómr, was instituted about A.D. 1004.

In this connection occurs the dura-dómr, or court at the door of the defendant, of which we have an accurate description in the Icelandic, and which, with the uproar which accompanied them would appear to have left their mark in the word durdom, or doordom, of our own dialect.

The dómhringr, or divisional law court, appeared to me to be so interesting, especially in the mode and manner in marking them out, that I wrote to Mr. Magnusson, who is a native Icelander, and has spent the whole of his earlier life in Iceland, to ask him whether there were any traces of these original courts yet to be found in that land. He wrote back and said that there were traces of them still be found scattered up and down that country.

The stone circles which are to be found scattered here and there in various parts of Cumberland and other portions of Lakeland have never, I think, been accounted for, nor has any hypothesis been brought forward that would more completely meet the case than the doom rings which marked the ancient law courts of the Norse.* They are called Druidical, certainly, by some writers, but I am not

---

* At a discussion which followed the reading of this paper at Sedbergh, it was remarked by some members of the Society that the date of the Cumberland megaliths was probably much earlier than the first immigration of the Norse. Without positively deciding either way, I may make the following quotation from Ferguson's *Northmen*. Speaking of Long Meg and her daughters, he says:— "Even if it could be shown to have been used by the Northmen it would not prove that they erected it, or if it could be proved to be of ancient British origin, would it show that they did not make use of it? For it would be as natural for the Northmen, finding such a magnificent structure ready made to their hand, to adopt it for their own purposes, as for the Moslems to convert the Christian Church of St. Sophia into a Mahommedan mosque."—T.E.

aware that there is anything, excepting mere hypothesis, to warrant the application of such a title as this. The earliest published account of them is by Camden, who made a survey of Cumberland in 1599; and the editor suggests that with regard to the stone circle at Little Salkeld, known as " Long Meg and her Daughters," that they were Norse in their origin, and were monuments used at the Investiture of Danish kings. A paper, entitled " A Group of Cumberland Megaliths," was read before the members of this Society on June 16th, 1880, by C. W. Dymond, in which he deals with and gives accurate plans and measurement of four such circles, namely, the one I have mentioned, known as Long Meg and her Daughters, the circles at Swinside and at Keswick, and the principal circle on Eskdale Moor. I have carefully read over all he has said about them, more especially what he has said about the stone circle at Keswick, and the long list of varied authorities he and other writers have quoted on the subject, and I cannot find any positive evidence for supposing that they were Druidical, rather than for supposing they were Norse. In the Orkney Islands the Standing Stones of Stennis, which are 70 or 80 in number, and form two circles of 100 feet and 360 feet in diameter, bear a strong resemblance to the stone circle at Keswick, there is no reason to suppose that the Druids ever occupied any part of the Orkneys, and tradition, as well as history, ascribes the stones of Stennis to the Scandinavians. I cannot see, therefore, why in those Domhringer, or Doom Circles, of the Landnama Book we may not find the origin or at any rate the use of those stone circles that are still existing amongst our own mountains, for I think I have shown with sufficient clearness that the same race, whose doings are recorded in the Landnama Book, came to Scotland and the northern portion of England at the same time that they went to Iceland, and it is well known that all those northern nations marked by such huge enclosures
their

their places of popular meeting, either for religious worship or for the transaction of public business of a temporal character ; and the passage itself seems to point out with sufficient clearness that such stone circles were used for purposes of judicial and religious assemblies, and had existed down to the time of the writer,· for the words— "Ok þar stendr enn þórs steinn, er þeir brutu þá menn um, er þeir blótudu, ok þar hjá er sá dómhringr, er menn skyldu till blóts dæma," are literally—

"There still stands the stone of Thor, over which they broke those men whom they sacrificed, and there is that Domhringr, or Doom-circle, where the people should be judged," *i.e.*, doomed, or condemned to sacrifice.

In a district that is very near to us, are preserved both the terms Dom and Thing, as applied to those assemblies. For the Deemster, or Doomster, of the Isle of Man was originally so-called because he pronounced doom or judgment in the legal assemblies, and the Tynwald Hill * (upon which the laws were promulgated) contains within it the root "þing," the title applied to the popular and legal assemblies of the Norse. In connection with these legal assemblies, I may note from the Landnama Book, his office who was the principal personage at such places, the Lögsögumadr, or law-speaker :—In the ancient Icelandic commonwealth, the community or State had its own laws, its own parliament, and its own lawsayer. This law-speaker was the first commoner, and the spokesman of the people at public assemblies and elsewhere. He was the guardian of the law, and the president of the legisla-

---

* The word Thingwald, or, as you give it, Tynwald, is preserved in a better form in Orkney and Shetland, where it is Thingwall; wall being the same as Icel. völlr (gen. vallar, dat. velli)=a field, Thingwall, therefore=Thingfield or Thing-mead.
You have Thingwall in Cheshire, Tinwald close by Dumfries in Scotland, where, too, on the Cromarty Firth, there is a Dingwall; in the neighbourhood of Whitby is a Thingwall.—E.M.

tive

tive body. As in heathen times, laws were not written ;
the law-speaker had to say what was the law of the land
in any case of doubt. In the general assemblies in Iceland he had to say the law from memory to the assembled
people from the law-hill ; hence in the Icelandic commonwealth he is called the law-speaker or law-sayer, and his
office law-speaking. As early Iceland was a commonwealth, the names and dates of those early law-speakers
are given in the Landnama Book in the very same way
that the names and dates of kings and their reigns are
given in other histories; one of the earliest and most
famed of them was Þorkell Máni, who held that office for
fifteen years, from A.D. 970. He was grandson of Ingolf the
first settler, and that is a most interesting passage in the
Landnáma Bók which describes his character and death.
It is as follows :—" Son Þorsteins var Þorkell máni lögsögumadr, einn heidinna manna hefir bezt verit siðaðr
at Þvi er menn vita dæmi til. Hann lét sik bera í
solargeisla í banasótt sinni, ok fal sik a hendi þeim guði
er sólina hafði skapat, hafði hann ok lifat sva hreinliga,
sem þeir kristnir menn er bezt eru siðaðir." I have thus
translated it :—

●

The son of Thorsteinn was Thorkell Moon, a lawspeaker, or lawsayer, who, so far as men can judge of exemplary conduct, was
the best of all the heathen folk. In his last illness he caused himself to be borne to where the beams of the sun shone upon him, and
commended himself, when so dying, into the hands of that god who
had shaped (skapat) the sun. His life had been pure as that of the
most religious of Christians.

Solar, the sun god, was an object of of worship amongst
the early Norsemen, and *Sunday* has a Norse as well as
an Anglo-Saxon significance. This passage shows very
plainly what they thought of their deity.

I am still dealing with the second extract which I have
translated from the Landnáma Bók, and wish to draw

your

your attention to one expressive word in that passage,
where it is said :—" Thorolf reared his homestead—the
words are in the original, þarr reisti hann bæ sinn—*there
raised he his dwelling.*" That word *dwelling*, in the
original Icelandic, is " bær"—b and æ dipthong ; the
word bæ is from the Icelandic " búa,"—to dwell, and
means, therefore, a dwelling; It is " Bö," in Norway ;
" By," in Denmark and Sweden, and the unnumbered
" bys" that we have as the termination of village names
in the north of England are really the " bær" that we
have in this passage of the Landnáma Bók and in the
map of northern England. The use of this word " By"
in the village and place-names may well serve to mark
out the limit and extent of the Norse immigration.
Anderson, our local dialect poet, who does not as a rule
go in much for derivation, has nevertheless noted the
frequent recurrence of this place-name, for in the
"Thuirsby Witch" he says :—

> There's Harraby an Tarraby,
> An Wigganby beseyde ;
> There's Oughterby an Souterby
> An " Bys" baith far and weyde.

A passage which occurs at page 126 of the Landnáma
Bók, gives an interesting instance of how this " bær" was
compounded as a proper name in Iceland. It is said of
Steinolf when he came to settle :—" Hann sá eitt rjódr í
dal þeim, þar lét hann bæ gjöra, ok kallaði Saurbæ, þvíat
þar var myrlent mjök, ok sva kallaði hann allan dalinn."
I have translated this as follows :—

He saw a clearing in the dale (otherwise grown with wood) and
there he built his bæ (dwelling), and called it Saurbæ—sour or
swampy dwelling, because there was much swampy land, and by the
same name he called the whole dale.

That is, he called the whole dale Saurbæ, or Sowerby,
the swampy dwelling. You will see this dale Saurbæ,
                                                    or

or Sowerby, marked upon this map of Iceland, and there is another instance upon this same map of precisely a similar application of the same name of Saurbær. Such swampy or boggy land is still called *sour* land in Cumberland, and with regard to this Saurbæ, or swampy dwelling, we have precisely the same name in Cumberland, in Sowerby, Castle Sowerby, and Temple Sowerby. Mȳr, or Mire, which also in this passage is used for boggy or swampy ground, has also illustrations in Cumberland, in " Mire"—Mire-House, Mire-Side, Pelutho-Mire, and The Mires. I have singled out the case of Saurbæ, or Sowerby, as an instance because in Iceland and in Cumberland the place-names derived therefrom are, as I may say, identical ; and it serves well to show from what natural circumstances the early Norsemen in both countries first fixed their dwellings, and named their homes.

From this verb " bua," to dwell or settle, we get another Norse word, "buandi," or "bondi,"* which meant *a tiller of the ground*, but always involved the idea of ownership, and hence especially marked the class represented in Cumberland, by the word " yeomen," who owned the land which they tilled.

In some cases in Iceland, as elsewhere, trees seem to have formed the origin of place-names, and in more instances than one, we find places in the Landnáma Bók called Reynir, or Reyni—this is almost without alteration, our Cumberland name of the mountain ash, or rowan tree ; the Danish brings it nearer still, it is rönne tree. Places in Iceland, therefore, called " Reynir," really mean the rowan trees,† or mountain ashes, and this word marks perhaps more than any other the intimate

---

* The surname " Bond" may have had its origin from this. —T.E.
† The fowler's service, mountain ash or rowan tree, one of the most elegant of British trees, conspicuous in the flowering season by its delicate green foliage and large bunches of blossom, and in autumn by its clusters of scarlet berries or pomes, used for catching birds ; hence one of its names.—T.E.

connection

connection between the words and superstitions of Scandinavia and the north of England. At p. 273 of the Landnáma Bók, it is applied in connection with a settlement as follows:—" Björn hét madr, audigr ok ofláti mikill, hann for til Íslands af Valldresi, ok nam land milli Kerlingarár ok Hafrsár, ok bjó at Reyni."

There was a man named Bjorn, opulent and very showy. He came to Iceland from Valldres, and took land between Kerling (Carline)-river, and Hafrs (Haver's) river, and dwelt at Reynir, or the Rowan trees.

It is also found in Rayni Keldur, or *the well at the rowan trees*, and Reyni Stadr. It was thus applied to mark places at the time of the settlement, as the only sort of tree, except the dwarf birch, to be found in Iceland. The rowan* was a holy tree, consecrated to Thor, and, according to the legends, to be found in their literature very intimately connected with the mysteries and superstitions of the Icelanders. " Raynir," from runa—a mystery, was so-called in Iceland from the supposed magical influence of the tree against witches.

---

* The sacredness of the rowan tree and the worship centring round it, was due to this myth:—Snorra Edda I., 286:—" Thor came to be a guest of the Ogress called Grídr, the mother of Vidar the Silent (dumb). She told Thor the truth of Geirröd. that he was a marvellously wise giant, and an evil one to deal with withal. She lent to Thor the belt of might and main (megingjardar) and iron grips, which were hers, and her staff, called Grid's staff, or pole. Then Thorir walked on to the river which is called Vimr, the greatest of all rivers. Then he clasped round himself the belt of might and main, and steadied himself against Grid's pole, which he stuck down water, but Loki held to the belt. And when Thor came to the middle of the river, then it waxed so greatly that it broke against the shoulder of him. Then sang Thor:—

Wax thou not, Wimur,
Awading as I am,
Unto the giants' homes.
Know, if thou waxest,
Then waxes, too, my might,
As high as the heaven's aloft.

Then saw Thor that, up in certain gorges, stood Gjalp, the daughter of Geirraud, astraddle across the river, and she it was that made the swelling of the river. Then Thor took a huge stone from the river bed, and hurled it at her, saying thus: at ouse (oyce=source) shall river be stemmed (stifled), nor did he miss his mark. And in the nick of time he staggered towards the bank, and caught hold of a certain rowan bush, and so stepped up out of the river. Hence the saying, " The Rowan the saving of Thor."—F.M.

There

There is a place called Raynors in Cumberland, which seems to mean "the mountain ashes." In some places in the north of England a piece of the rowan tree used to be placed above the door to scare away evil influences, and in Lakeland the stick for stirring the cream is frequently of rowan tree wood, to counteract the malign spiritual influences which at times bewitched the churn, so that no butter was forthcoming. This idea is found in Burns where he says:—

> Thence country wives in toil and pain,
>   May plunge and plunge the kirn in vain ;
> For, oh ! the yellow treasures taen
>   By witching skill,
> And dawtit twal-pint hawkies gaen
>   As yells the bill.

Anent this supposed magical influence of the rowan tree, Will Ritson, of Wasdale Head, once told me the following story :—

It has from time immemorial been the custom of the people of Wasdale to carry their dead to Eskdale or Netherwasdale Church for interment, there being no burial ground attached to the church at Wasdale Head. The corpse in the coffin is slung over the back of a horse and carried in this fashion over the fell. On one occasion (lang sen) the wife of a dalesman was being so carried for interment. When upon the edge of the fell the coffin, through the negligence of the driver of the horse, came in contact with a rowan tree, and was thrown to the ground. By the concussion the coffin was forced open, and the supposed corpse was found to be alive. She returned home with her friends, and lived for several years after. When she died, and the same kind of cavalcade was following her remains in very much the same fashion, as they approached the said rowan tree again, her husband, who was bringing up the rear, called out (according to Will) in stentorian tones : " Tak' care o' that rowan tree !" This time, however, the rowan tree was successfully cleared.

At p. 109 of the Landnáma Bók is the record of the settlement of a Norsewoman named Aud. She was the

wife

wife of Olaf the White, King of Dublin.   Upon his death
she went with her son Thorsteinn, and settled in the
Hebrides.   Thence her son, joining with Sigard, subdued
Caithness, Sutherland, Ross, and Murray, and in all
more than half of. Scotland.   He was slain in battle.
She then sailed for Iceland, as is recorded in the following passage :—" Eptir þat for Audr at leita Islands : hun
hafði á Skipi með sér xx karla frjálsa."   This passage
may be rendered :—"After that Audr went to seek Iceland ; she had in the ship with her 20 freemen :—

Taking this sentence word for word there is a remarkable correspondence between it and our northern dialect,
and the old words that still linger on in the translation of
the Bible, as the older and purer form of Early English
speech :—*Epter þat*—after that needs no translation ; *for*,
or *fare*, means " to go," in the Icelandic ; we have the
very word in " farewell—go well.   In Genesis the same
old word occurs—" See how the brethren *fare*"—" See how
they go."   At leita, "to seek," is a phrase we have in
North Lancashire ; anybody in Furness knows just as well
as they know in Iceland that " at lait"=to seek.   "*In a
skipi*," in the ship, *a* means *on* or *in*, and is really the very
same *a* that we have in the old phrases abroad—*a*stern,
*a*foot : *karl*, a man of lower degree, or freed man ; we have
the very same word in the Bible in the phrase, " Nor the
churl said to be bountiful."—Isaiah xxxii.

Thus far then the account of Audr's going to Iceland.
She spent an active and eventful life there, and at p. 117
of the Landnáma Bók, we have the following record of
her death :—

Audr was a very noble lady,* and when she was weary with eld
(old age) she invited her kinsmen and folk-in-law, and made ready a

---

* Aud was third in descent from Ingolf, the original settler of Iceland, and was
ancestress of Ari, compiler of the Landnama Book, who claims to be eighth in
descent from her.—T.E.

grand banquet. And when the banquet had lasted for three nights, then she selected gifts for her friends, and also gave them wholesome counsel. She said that the banquet should still last for another three nights, and she added that that should be her funeral banquet (Erfi). The night after this she died, and was buried in the space upon the seashore between high and low water marks (flædarmali) as she had given directions; because she would not lay in unconsecrated ground, (moldu), since she was baptised.

The following is the passage in the original Icelandic :—

" Audr *var* vegskona *mikil, þá* er *hún var* ellimóð, *bauð hun til* sín *frændum* sínum ok mágum ok bjo dijrlega veizla ; en er þrjár *nætr* hafði veizlan staðit, *þá valdi hún gjafir* vinum sínum ok réð þeim *heilrædi* ; *sagði hún* at *þá skyldi standa* veizlan enn iii *nætr* ; *hún kvað þat vera skyldu erfi* sitt ; *þá nótt eptir* andaðist *hún*, ok *var grafin í flædarmáli*, sem *hún hafði fyrir sagt, þvíat hún uildi* sigi *liggja* í óvígðri *moldu*, er *hún uar* skírð."*

" Baud," invited, in this passage corresponds with the old word " bid," last *bad*, or *bade*, which was used for inviting to a funeral, and the district of those invited was, and sometimes still is in Cumberland, called a " bidding." We have the same old word in the Liturgy, in the bidding or invitatory prayer.

" Mold," the word here used for earth in the burial, finds a parallel in a Cumberland phrase for " inter," which is *to put in the mould* :—Flædarmá, is the space between high and low water marks, and, I may remark, as a parallel to this case of Audr, the superstition that has so often prevailed in Cumberland in individuals as to whether they would or would not be interred in consecrated ground.

" Flædar" is the gen. of flædr, *f.*, the flood or high tide.

---

* In this Icelandic passage I have put in italics every word that seems allied to, or identical with, the dialect. They amount in this short passage to thirty-seven. —T.E.

It

It is in other parts of Iceland called " Flöd," and on the
Cumberland shores of the Solway the tide was, since I
remember, in some parts always spoken of as the *flood*.
"Valdi," here used, means in Icelandic *to select*. We
have the same word in the dialect in *weel, to pick out* or
select, as of apples, the sortings of which are called " out-
weels."

The word " Erfi," which is used in the original as the
name of this funeral banquet is, I think, worthy of note in
this connection :—Arfr, meant the inheritance or patri-
mony, and " arf-sal" was a law term, signifying the hand-
ing over of one's property to another man on condition of
getting succour or support for life.   Hence Audr's funeral
banquet, under the name " erfi," was a sort of passing
over of her possessions to her heirs and successors, and
finds an exact correspondence in what was called the
" arval," or funeral banquet in Cumberland and North
Lancashire, where the friends and neighbours of the
family of the deceased were invited to dinner on the day
of the interment, and this was called the " arval dinner,"
a solemn festival to exculpate the heir and those entitled
to the possessions of the deceased from the mulcts or
fines of the lord of the manor, and from all accusation of
having used violence.

In later times the word acquired a wider application,
and was used to designate the meals provided at funerals
generally ; and this word, the arval, or funeral dinner,
has in the dialect come down nearly to our own time.

Mr. Magnússon kindly sent me a note upon this subject, in which he says that " arval" has its nearest etymo-
logical equivalent in modern Danish " arveöl," from the
old form *arfa öl*=the inheritors' ale.

With regard to place-names, there is a remarkable
correspondence in form and meaning between the place-
names of Iceland and those of the three northern counties
which I have especially named in my paper.

I

I have said that there are in all 1,949 place-names, or farm-names, in the list at the end of the Landnáma Bók. Some of these must be discounted as applying to other countries or districts than Iceland, but after all a very great proportion remain of what are purely Icelandic place-names ; and in addition to this I have here a large map of Iceland as it was in the twelfth century, and this will, therefore, serve to illustrate that period of the Landnáma Bók. I have copied those place-names as fully as I could, and they correspond in a remarkable degree to the place-names that we find in Cumberland, Westmorland, and North Lancashire.

Ness, Frith, Vik,* and Sand, fringe every portion of the map of Iceland. " Dale," is found continually in Iceland, —Broad-dale, Lang-dale, Deep-dale, Reek-dale, and Swin-dale are instances, some of which occur more than once. Anent this last name Swindale, as we have it also in Lakeland, it may not be uninteresting to read why the Icelandic Swindale was first so named. The following passage occurs at p. 177 of the Landnáma Bók :—" Ingimund lost ten swine, and found them in the autumn of the following year in Swindale, where there were then one hundred swine." It goes on to speak about the boar leaping into a pool, called therefrom " Swine's Pool." The Icelandic word here used for " boar" is significant, for it is *göltr* for the masculine, *gyltr* for the feminine, and in Cumberland a young swine is still called a gilt pig.

Thor gives the origin to numerous place-names and surnames, as will be especially illustrated by some of the passages I have illustrated.

In Iceland, as in Cumberland, there is a kaldá, or cold stream. There is also in Iceland the White river and

---

* " Vik" is a bight or bay, and a glance at the Ordnance Map will show that it is used once or twice in this sense in the bays or openings on the Lake of Windermere.—T.E.

Laxá

Laxá,* or the salmon river, and those bearing the name of *sands and skerries* seem to be as numerous as those to be found upon our own shores. The kind of dwelling they originally built in the settlement there, as here, sometimes goes to form the name.

Thus there is Tentstead and Tentness, as in Lakeland we have Tent Lodge and Tent Cottage. The word "skali," in the Icelandic meant a shed, a hut—the Engl. sheal, shealing, and as such it seems to form the original of several place-names in Iceland. We have it also as a common noun in Lakeland for a similar shed or enclosure, for storing turf is called a peat-scale, and the Skalafell, Skalawood, Skalamyre, and Skalanes of Iceland, may remind us of the Scales—Geitscale, Nether Scales, Scale Hill, and Bowscale of our own land.

"Gard" is an enclosure; we have it as a common noun in the Bible of Ulphilas, where in the 10th John sheepfold is translated gardr; and gard, or gardr, as an enclosure, occurs in many place-names in the map of Iceland, and is represented by proper names in "gards" and "garth," to be found very frequently in our own neighbourhood, and Stackgarth and Kurkgarth, used as common nouns in our dialect, correspond in sound and meaning with Stackgard and Kurkgard in Iceland.

There is a Kirkfell in Iceland, as in Lakeland, and there are names that remind us of their demons as well as of their divinities. "Troll" is their name for fiend or giant, and Trollsheim and Trollsdwelling, as they are applied to the Icelandic mountains, remind us of the supposed whereabouts of those fiends or giants, and Fiends' Fell, the former name of Cross Fell, supplies a parallel from our own mountains; and there is a bay called Ker-

---

* Laxa, or salmon river, may remind us of Laxey in the Isle of Man. "Lax" is the Icelandic for salmon, and till lately salmon weirs were at times called *lax* weirs in the north of England.—T.E.

linger

linger, or Old Woman's, or Witches Frith, because (says
the Landnáma Bók) when Eysteinn, the son of Thorsteinn, attempted to land there, a witch drove his ship
back into the frith. This word "kerling" has found a
habitat in the north of our island, for in Scotland the word
"karline" is an old woman or witch. "Gufa," in Icelandic, is steam or vapour, and occurs in Gufu nes, Gufu
dale, and Gufu scale—proper names which doubtless
derive their origin from the steam or hot wells in the
neighbourhood. The modern Icelandic preserves it in
Gufa-batr, a steamboat, and a vapouring fellow in Cumberland used to be called a great " guff."

I have been speaking of proper names. I may say a
word in conclusion about what I suppose would not
inaptly be called improper names. The Landnáma Bok
abounds in nick-names, every kind of personal pecu-
liarity, almost every shade of complexion, every kind of
defect and deformity, a man's tidiness or untidiness,
whether he was long or short, fat or lean, flat-footed or
the opposite, good, bad, or indifferent—all seem to have
been represented by an epithet placed immediately after
his baptismal name, and in that position as a personal
appellative to have stuck on to him through life. It
stuck to him better than a degree sticks to some people,
and in many instances in the Landnáma Bók it would
seem to be the only name by which he was generally
known. Anyone who knew the Cumberland villages forty
or fifty years ago, or earlier still, needs not to be reminded
that in this particular they were not far behind the
Norsemen. Anderson's " Kursmas Eve" or Mark Lonsdale's " Upshot" supply such Cumberland nicknames in
abundance. This last is the free sketch of a Cumberland
upshot, and was taken in 1780. In the notes upon the
original edition of the "Upshot" there is the following
reference to these nicknames :—" These bye-titles are so
far from giving offence that the parties themselves admit
them

them on all occasions, and sometimes use them in writing."

In some villages there was hardly a person who was not designated by such an epithet, and as in Iceland it got to be almost the only name by which he was known. A careful analysis and comparison of some of those names in Iceland shows that in some instances they became surnames, and in the case of their posterity they were handed down as the only family surname by which their descendants were known.

One nickname in the Landnáma Bók reminds us of a very curious custom in Iceland. There are three men spoken of there whose nicknames are Hólmgöngu Starri, Hólmgöngu Mani, and Hólmgöngu Rafn. They were so named because they had fought in the Holmgang. This Holmgang was the Icelandic wager of battle. The combatants went alone to a holm or island, and fought until one of them was wounded or dead. The holm gang was therefore a kind of court of final appeal or ordeal, and whenever a Thing or parliament was assembled, an islet or holm was appointed near to it as the place for the holm gang or wager of battle, and throughout the Landnáma Bók it is spoken of as something well known and admitted. About A.D. 1006 this wager of battle or holm gang was abolished on account of an unfortunate feud between two of their well known leaders. The word " holm," is apparently as a proper and a common noun, used as generally in Iceland as in Lakeland, and it has in both cases exactly the same meaning, namely, that of an islet, especially in a bay, creek, or river, and even meadows on the shore with ditches behind them are, in both countries, called holmes.

Such then is some of the evidence, however imperfectly rendered, that I have to tender of the affinities between the Language, Place-names, Folklore, and Antiquities derived from the oldest and best authenticated record of

the

the ancient Norsemen, and the Language, Place Names, Folklore, and Antiquities of those three countries in which your Society carries on its valuable and interesting work. Icelandic is certainly the most unchanged and characteristic form of the language of the Norsemen. The Landnama Book is the truest type of its earliest records, and the writers of it are placed in the very front rank of their historians.

I have done what little I could to translate some portion of that record, and I hope that abler hands, with greater resources, may soon translate the whole of it with an especial view to showing its bearing upon the Dialect, Place-names, and Folklore of our northern counties.

But with what I have done, I have little hesitation in saying that the language of our three northern counties, so far as it is or has been a distinctive language, is founded upon a Norse original, that our place-names have the most close and striking affinities and at times also identities with the place-names of Iceland, as recorded in the Landnama Book. That the Scandinavian mythology enters very largely into our folklore and superstitions, and that the unwritten history contained in the stones and megaliths to be found upon our mountains, will, as it is better interpreted, point still more and more clearly to the doom circles and religious places of assembly that were first founded by the Norse.

———

The Chronology of the Icelandic Commonweath as given in the Landnama Book.

THE names of some of the leading Norse settlers in Iceland have been given in the proceeding paper and also the omens by which they were led to take possession of a claim.

Those who went from the British Islands seem to have been in a great measure related or connected by marriage. Those Norse chiefs solemnly took possession of the land,* or as it may be explained, consecrated it to their own use in the name of the Divinity.

After this, in order to found a community, they built a temple and called themselves by the name Godi or Hof-Godi, *i.e.*, Temple Priest. ' The temple became the centre of the new community and the founder was, in civil matters, their chieftain and in religious matters, their priest.

Many independent chieftains or liege lords thus sprung up through the country until the year 930, when the Althing was established where all the petty chiefs entered into a kind of league and laid the foundation of a general goverment for the whole island. This Althing was the Parliament or general assembly of the Icelandic Common wealth and was invested with supreme legislative and judicial power.

Under this government somewhat changed when Christianity was introduced, the Icelandic Commonwealth existed for about three hundred years.

The central figure of this community was the Lawman.

---

* Several modes of taking possession are instanced in the passages I have quoted elsewhere such as the drifting ashore of the High Seat Post, naming the land which was a religious ceremony, and hallowing the land by fire.

He

He was the Guardian of the Law and the President of the Legislation Assembly and of the Law Courts.

As in heathen times the laws were not written, the Lawman had to say what was the law of the land in any cases of doubt.

In the general assemblies in Iceland, he had to say the law of the land to the assembled people—from the Law Hill—hence in the Icelandic Commonwealth he is called the Lawspeaker or Lawsayer, and his office is called Lawspeaking.

For the first one hundred years (930 to 1030) he was elected for life, afterwards for a shorter period.

The following are the chief dates of the Settlement and of the Commonwealth as given in the Landnama :—

A.D.

852—The Norse Sea King Olave the White landed at Dublin and founded a Norse Principality.

875—Ingolf first settled Iceland.

884—Thorolf Mostbeard first took land at Thorsness.

892 (about)—Queen Aud came to Iceland and settled all the Dale lands.

927—Ulfljotr brought a system of law from Norway to Iceland. He first promulged a system of law in Iceland and by his advice the Althing was established.

930—The Althing is inaugurated : Rafn son of Ketil the Salmon first had the office of Lawspeaker and said law for 20 years.

950—Thoravinn Ragabrodir son of Olaf was Lawspeaker for 20 years.

970—Thorkell Mani Thorsteinnson was Lawspeaker for about 15 years.

985—Thorgeirr Thorkell's son was Lawspeaker for 17 years.

1000—Christianity introduced into Iceland. Discovery of Vineland or America by the Norsemen.

1002—Grimr Sversting's son from Mossfell was Lawspeaker about 2 years.

1004—Skapti son of Thorodd the Priest was Lawspeaker about 26 years. He died in the same year in which St. Olave the King fell, about 1030.

1031—Steinn Thorgest's son was Lawspeaker for 3 years.

1034—Thorkell was Lawspeaker (the second time) for 19 years.

1054—Gellir Bolverk's son was Lawspeaker for 9 years.
1056—Isleif was consecrated first Bishop of Iceland at Skalholt.
1063—Gunnarr the prophet Thorgrim's son was Lawspeaker 3 years.
1066—Kolbein Flosason was Lawspeaker 6 years. That summer King Harald Sigurd's son fell in England.
1071—Gellir was Lawspeaker the second time for 3 years.
1075—Gunnarr Lawspeaker the second time for 1 year.
1076—Sighvatr Lawspeaker for 8 years.
1080—Gellir Lawspeaker third time.
1084—Markas Skeggjason Lawspeaker that summer and died 1093.
1093—Bergthorr Hrafnsson was Lawspeaker.
1097—Tuindargjald took law to Iceland.
1107—Ulfedinn took law to Iceland.
1106—Bergthorr Lawspeaker (second time). About this time the Christian Scriptures were brought to Iceland.
1122—Gudmundr Thorgeirr's son was Lawspeaker 17 years.
1139—Rafn Ulfhedin's son Lawspeaker 4 years.
1143—Finnr Hallsson 6 years.
1149—Rafn Ulfhedin's son 10 years.
1159—Snorri Lawspeaker 15 years.
1174—Styrkarr Oddason 10 years.
1184—Gizür Hallson 22 years.
1206—Hallr Gizurason Lawspeaker 8 years.
1214—Styrmir Karason Lawspeaker 5 years.
1219—Snorri Sturluson Lawspeaker 4 years.
1223—Teitr Thorvalds son 3 years.
1226—Snorri Sturluson (second time) Lawspeaker 10 years.
1236—Strymir Karason second time 4 years.
1240—Teitr Thorvald's son second time 12 years.
1252—Olafr Thordarson Lawspeaker 3 years.
256—Olafr Thordarson second time 1 year.
257—Teitr Einar's son lawspeaker 6 years.
1262—Final submission of Iceland to the King of Norway.

As the Icelandic Commonweath rose and was formed by the families of whom the Landnama Book describes the settlement, namely, in a great measure by the families of Ingolf, Thorolf, Queen Aud and her very numerous connexions and descendants, so with the Sturlung Family, who at that time represented all that was distinguished in intellect in literature and in political influence, we have the era of its decline and fall.

A

A brief notice therefore of Snorri Sturluson, the last of the three brothers representing this family, may fitly form the conclusion of the chronological table which I have here given.

Snorri Sturluson was born in 1178 at Hvamma* where his family, who traced their descent to the ancient Kings of Norway, had been settled since the first colonization of the island.

Hvamma was the home of Aud about whom so much has been said, and who came from Britain as one of the original settlers of the island. And throughout the times of the Commonwealth this same farm of Hvamma continued to be a great centre of intellectual and political influence and life. Snorri was placed at an early age under the care of Ion Loptson, son of Sigfusson, the learned compiler of the old Edda, by whom he was instructed in the history, mythology, and poetry of the north as well as in classical literature. By his marriage at the age of twenty-six with a rich heiress, and the early death of his father, he soon attained to a position of wealth and influence, and, as will be seen from the foregoing Table, was twice elected to be Lawsayer or Supreme Magistrate of the Island. In this post he was distinguished for his profound knowledge of the laws and civil institutions of his native country; but his ambition, avarice, and love of intrigue embroiled him personally in sanguinary feuds, and contributed much to hasten the destruction of Icelandic independence. His love of intrigue led him to take part in the intestine troubles of Norway, and thus drew upon him the suspicion and ill will of the Norwegian King Hakon, who sent secret instructions for his arrest and if need be for his assassination. The King's intentions were carried out to their

---

* See a notice of this word in the vocabulary of Fell, Field, and Farm names at the end of this volume.

fullest

fullest extent, and his numerous enemies joining together
in a plot against him, he was attacked in his own house
and murdered in the year 1241. His death was literally
an illustration of the truth that a man's foes shall be they
of his own household, for the leaders of his murderers
were Gizur and Arni, his sons in-law, whose influence
with the Kings of Norway had been the direct cause of
his death. He exercised as great an influence over the
literary as over the political History of Iceland. He
was a poet of no mean order, and composed poems on
the Kings and Jarls at whose court he had sojourned.
His great work, however, is the Heimskringla or History
of the Kings of Norway from the earliest times to the
death of Erlingsson in 1177, and which he compiled from
ancient genealogical tables and other documents. This
work is now being translated into English by Eric
Magnusson, and brought out in the volumes of " The
Saga Library." The death of Snorri marks the fall of the
Icelandic Commonwealth, for the remaining portion of its
history is little more than a series of reprisals between his
avengers and their opponents. It includes the burning of
Flumyra and the slaughter of the Burners. At the return
of Earl Gizur from Norway, whither he had gone to
receive the title of Earl, the final submission of Norway
took place in 1262, when the remaining two quarters and
a half of the Island took the oath of allegiance to the
King of Norway, consented to pay him tribute, and to
come under the government of an Earl. The history of
the decline and fall of the Independent Icelandic Commonwealth is told in the Icelandic Saga of Sturla Thordsson, who was himself contemporary with the concluding
portion of it, and a member of the Sturlung Family, and
who, having been present at some of the most terrible
incidents that mark the Fall of the Commonwealth, describes them with a vividness and reality which could not
have been expected from anyone else.

His

His whole history as contained in the Icelandic Saga extends from A.D. 1196 to 1262, and takes in the feuds which existed from 1208 until 1258, a period of 50 years. The fall of the Commonwealth and the destruction of those old houses whose origin is given in the Landnama is what that history or Saga really means. For some years during the concluding portion of this war the Chiefs of Houses had one by one been giving up their rule and sending in their submission to Norway; the Chiefs of the leading factions had almost exterminated each other in their various hand to hand encounters. The Island as Thordsson describes it was thus in some measure rendered powerless to cope with its outside enemies, who in assisting the Icelanders against each other had been acting on the principle of " Divide et impera," so that the final submission of the Feudal chieftains as they one after another took the oath of allegiance, consented to pay tribute and resigned their rule to the King of Norway was really but the necessary outcome of this long and disastrous internal war.

The Folklore of Lakeland and Iceland.

THE Icelandic Landtake, as will be seen from the evidence already adduced, was almost entirely directed by omens.

The Norse settlers at times made the most trivial circumstances guide them in the selection of their future homes.

In one instance the flight of ravens directed an early discoverer to his landing place; in another, when a chieftain who was leading an expedition died on board, then his sons threw overboard the coffin * in which his body had been placed; to guide them to their future settlement, and at p. 76 of the Landnama, a Mermennil or Merman, which had been brought up in fishing, is made to point out in a somewhat enigmatical manner the position of a settler's Landtake and the place where his abode shall be built.

The casting overboard of the High Seat Pillar seems, however, to have been by much the most general and recognised method of directing a Landtake, and the Landtake of Thorolf Mostbeard as so directed exercised a most lasting influence upon the history and institutions of the Island. This took place A.D. 884 or just ten years after the arrival of Ingolf, the original settler. I have already (pages 8-11) quoted the recital of Thorolf's landing and of his calling the fell upon the ness where the pillar came to land Helgafell, or the Holy Hill. The Eyrbyggja Saga, chapter 4, contains an account of the temple which he reared in this place. "There," it is said, "he built a temple, and a mighty house it was. There was a door in

---

* The word used really implies something larger than a coffin, evidently something that would float the body until it came to land.

the

the side wall, and nearer to the end thereof. Within the door stood the pillars of the high seat, and nails were therein. They were called the god's nails. Off the inmost house was another house, of the fashion of the choir of a church, and a stall or altar, with a ring weighing 20 ounces laid upon it, and upon this ring men were required to swear all the oaths. At all public meetings the chief was required to have this ring upon his arm. On the stall or altar stood the blood bowl, and therein was the blood rod, which was like unto a sprinkler, and therewith should be sprinkled from the bowl that blood which is Hlaut, which was that kind of blood which flowed when those beasts were smitten which were sacrificed to the gods. But round about the stall were the gods arranged in the Holy Place."

THE NORSE OATH.

The form of this Norse oath upon the Ring is given in the Landnama Book, at page 259, as follows:—Every man who was there to transact any business as by law provided before the Court, should first take an oath upon that ring, and name for the purpose two or more witnesses and repeat the following words:—I call witnesses in evidence that I take oath upon the Ring. A lawful oath (lögeid) so help me Freya and Niord and the Almighty God, as I shall in this case—prosecute or defend or bear witness or give sentence or pronounce doom according as I know what is most right and most true and most lawful and that I will deal lawfully with all such matters as come under my jurisdiction while I am at this Thing.'

THE HOLY HILL.

The sacred character of the mountain where Thorolf first landed and its connexion with the religious belief of the Norsemen is well marked in the following extract
from

from the Landnama :—" Thorolf took land (land nam) from Staffriver inward to Thorsriver and called all that part Thorsness.   He had so great a reverence for that fell which stands upon the ness, and which he called Helga Fell, Holy Hill, that he ordained that thither should no man unwashen look ; and there was so great a place-hallowedness (sanctuary) that nothing should be destroyed upon the mountain, neither cattle nor people unless it should go away of its own accord.   That was the belief of Thorolf and his kinsmen that they should die into the mountain."   This passage shows, therefore, that the Holy Hill where Thor's High Seat or Pillar came ashore was thereby consecrated as a place of sanctuary or refuge.   The most hallowing influence, however, connected with this sacred mountain would be doubtless in the idea contained in the last sentence I have quoted, viz. :—It was the belief of Thorolf and his kinsmen that *they should die into the mountain, i.e.,* that they should dwell within the mountain after their death.   It is an advantage to rightly understanding this passage that the Eyrbyggja Saga in its first twelve chapters deals almost exclusively with Thorolf, his landing, his form of religious worship, and his descendants.   Chapter 11 of this Saga when describing the death of Thorsteinn the son of Thorolf Most-beard, the original settler, gives such a graphic account of what is meant by *" Die into the mountain,"* that I have thought it well to quote it in full.   It seems to me to afford a remarkable parallel to that well-known Cumberland superstition which used to be so well known as

THE FOREBODING OR FOREWARNING OF DEATH.

I subjoin a translation of the passage* :—" That same

---

* The student who is comparing the Icelandic with North English will do well to read this passage in Icelandic.   It will be found at p. 88 of Vigfusson and Powell's Icelandic Reader (Clarendon Press, 1879).

harvest Thorsteinn went out to Hoskulds Island to lay in stores (of fish), and it chanced that one evening in that harvest that a shepherd of Thorsteinn went to look after his flock to the north of the Holy Hill.   He observed that the fell opened out towards the north end and within the fell he saw mighty fires and could hear a great noise there and the clanging of drinking horns.   And he listened if he could catch any distinct words and he heard that they were greeting Thorsteinn and his seafaring companions and bidding him to sit in the High Seat over against his father (Thorolf Mostbeard).   This forewarning the shepherd told to Thora, the wife of Thorsteinn, in the evening. She spake little about it but said that it might be the foreboding of heavier tidings.   The morning after men came out from Hoskulds Island, and told those tidings that Thorsteinn Codbiter had been drowned whilst fishing, and men regarded this as a great disaster."

HALLOWING THE LAND BY FIRE

seems to have been a frequent method of defining the Icelandic Landtake and the origin of this is pointed out at page 276 of the Landnama—part V., cap. I.   " Those who came out afterwards thought that the earlier settlers had taken too great an extent of land into their own possession but Harald the Fair-haired, made them agree to this, that no one should have a wider extent of land than he himself and his companions from the ship could carry fire across in one day.   They should make fires when the sun was in the east, and also they should make other smokes, so that they could see the one from the other ; and that those fires which they made when the sun was in the east should burn until nightfall, so they should go until the sun was in the west and then make other fires." *

---

* The limits of their claims therefore would be so far as from one extremity they could see the smokes raised at the other extremity by day or the fires by night.

An

An example of how those directions were carried out is given at page 207 of the Landnama, where there is a notice of Helgi the Lean, a settler from the western islands of Scotland as follows:—" Helgi searched the whole district during that summer and took possession of all Eyiafiord between Sigluness and Reynisness and made a large fire at every river mouth and consecrated to himself all the district. He resided that winter at Bildsa, and in spring he made his dwelling (bu) in Christness, and dwelt there for the rest of his life." The Helgi here mentioned was brother-in-law to Queen Aud who with the various members of her kindred makes much the most important figure in the Settlement and early History of Iceland, and I think it is most important to be noted that all this band of settlers, though almost entirely composed of Noremen, came last from the British Islands and seem to have kept up a connexion and correspondence therewith.

There is a passage at page 193 of the Landnama which not only gives a remarkable instance of this custom of fire-hallowing but also records an example of Norse sharp practice in obtaining the first possession of a claim of land. It is there said :—" There was a man named Onund the Wise who took land (land nam) up from Mark Gill along all the eastern side of the valley, but when Eric (named in a former chapter) would go and settle the western side of that valley, then Onund made a forecast by sacrifice that he might know at what time Eric would go and take possession of the dale, and Onund was the quicker and shot across the river with a tinder-arrow or fire arrow and hallowed for himself the land on the western side of the river and built his dwelling beside the river."

It is very probable that Onund took his title of the Wise from the adroitness which he manifested on this ocasion, for the word viss (wise) which describes his *knowing* in such a way as to anticipate the landtake of Eric, is also the title given to him as Onund the Wise.   The

The signal fires which have been spoken of as passed
on from claim to claim by the Norsemen in Iceland in
evidence of hallowing or appropriating those claims find a
parallel in the Bale* fires or signal fires which were once
so well known more especially in the north.

"The Beacon" is used as the name of several hills in the
Lake District, and there seems to be no doubt that the
name took its first origin from the signal or beacon fires,
which were lighted upon those hills in time of danger,
each district having one of its own, the names of a range
of such fire stations extending across Lakeland are still
preserved, and they have been used occasionally, even
down to more modern times.

FAIRYLAND.

There is a word used in connexion with the establishment
of the Quarter Thing on Thorsness, by Thorolf, which
when closely considered throws great light upon the early
superstitions of Iceland. That word is Alfrek and is
applied therein to any influence which may drive away
the guardian spirits from the land.

The word itself tells as much, Alf being equivalent to
elves or guardian deities or "the good folk," and "reck,"
as I have elsewhere noted, comes from the verb rekkan,
to drive, which we have in such words as rack, wreck, &c.

In Icelandic, Alfr, in Danish, Ellefolk, and in Swedish,
Elf, all represent elves or fairies, a class of benign guardian spirits the belief in which seems to have been very
closely bound up with the folk lore and superstitions which
the Landnama Book contains or implies. At page 258
occurs a passage on this subject of which the subjoined is a

---

* Dr. Whitaker and other writers after him have suggested that Hill Bell, between Troutbeck and Kentmere, took its name from sacrifices being offered upon
it or fires being lighted upon it, to Belus or Baal, the Babylonian or Syrian God.
Surely if fire has anything to do with the derivation of the name, the Bale fires of
the Norsemen, which were probably lighted upon it, suggest a much more
obvious derivation of the name.

paraphrase

paraphrase, or at any rate a very free translation. " There
was a heathen law passed at the time of the Settlement
that intending settlers should not have carved figure
heads upon the stem of their ships when at sea. But if
they had such carved figureheads they should take them
off before they came within sight of land so that they
might not sail to land having in front of them gaping
figure heads or grinning beaks, lest they should drive
away the guardian spirits of the land." *

Now these guardian or protecting influences which
were so liable to be driven away by the Alfrek, mentioned
in connexion with the early settlement, or by the gaping
and grinning figure heads carved upon the war ships of
the Norsemen, seem to be peculiar to the Scandinavian as
distinguished from the Classical Mythology, and under the
names of elves or fairies to have come in our own folk
lore very nearly down to within living memory. In a
country which abounded in natural and unexplained
phenomena, where the geysir and the volcano, especially
as seen and heard though the long lone nights of an
Arctic winter must have brought the unexplored world
within a measureable distance, Shadowland and Fairy-
land doubtless appeared much more vividly and distinctly
than they do in other countries, yet any native of our
northern counties who will read carefully over the Landnama must find therein much to remind him of the fairy
folk lore which he has almost imperceptibly imbibed in
his earlier years.

---

* Land vaettr,—guardian spirits of the land; a further account of them is
given at p. 271, where it is said of a settler :—" Bjorn dreamed one night that a
giant (literally ' a rock dweller ') came to him and bade him enter into partner-
ship with him, and Bjorn assented to his proposal. After that it is related that
his cattle increased so rapidly that he was speedily rolling in riches. Then, on
account of a mysterious wild buck that came to his flock he was nick-named Hafr
Bjorn, or Bjorn Wild Buck, and men who had the power of second sight (ghost
seers) observed this that the guardian spirits of the land (land vaettr,—elves or
fairies) followed Bjorn to the Thing and that they followed Thorsteinn and Thord
in hunting and fishing."

There

There is the mermennil or merman appearing and pro-
phesying their fate to the early Norse settlers, and I think
many of the older amongst our number will be able to
remember a time when they were tanght legends about
mermaids which at critical times, as storms at sea, came
up and foretold the fate of sailors, clothing their remarks
in enigmatical or mysterious words.

And with regard to fairies and guardian spirits, they
seem to be adopted as a portion of their creed by the
compilers of the Landnama, and no one there doubts their
existence, and half a century ago in rural districts in
Scotland and Cumberland those Green men or Fairies were
an undoubted article of belief. I never saw them certainly, but as a boy I firmly believed in their existence. I
believed, and my belief was formed from the teaching of
those learned in folk lore, that the fairies often came forth
and joined their revels in obscure thickets and remote
grassy dells, and if a disbeliever wished to have his
doubts settled upon the subject he could be referred to the
visible testimony of those circles known as Fairy Rings.*

---

* The following admirable description of the Edenhall "Fairies round their
Fairy King" is evidently the account of one skilled in fairy lore :—

> Twelve hundred elfin knights and more
> Were there in silk and steel arrayed,
> And each a ruby helmet wore,
> And each a diamond lance displayed.

> And pursuivants with wands of gold,
> And minstrels scarf'd and laurelled fair;
> Heralds with blazoned flags unrolled,
> And trumpet-tuning dwarfs were there.

> Behind twelve hundred ladies coy
> On milk-white steeds brought up their Queen;
> Their 'kerchiefs of the crimson soy,
> Their kirtles all of Lincoln green.

> Some wore, in fanciful costume,
> A sapphire or a topaz crown,
> And some a hern or peacock's plume,
> Which their own tercel knights struck down.

> And some wore masks, and some wore hoods,
> Some turbans rich, some onches rare;
> And some sweet woodbine from the woods,
> To bind their undulating hair.

But

But where did those fairies come from? and where did they go to? Once suppose an underground world and you have not the least difficulty in getting over this aspect of the question, and an underground world was a firm belief in our northern folk lore just as it was a firm belief in the folk lore and superstitions which are disclosed by the Landnam and other Sagas of the Norse. Thorolf and his descendants believed that they should die into the mountain to which his High Seat Pillar had directed him when he came to Iceland as a settler, and when his herdsman on the night of Thorsteinn's death was shepherding upon the same mountain, he saw the whole of it opened towards the north and lighted up, and heard the revellers within that mountain welcoming Thorsteinn to the higher seat at their festive board; also doubtless the mysterious guardian spirits that came among men were understood to disappear into the earth. They had the same jealous character in the north of England that they had in Iceland, and any malign or counteracting influence was sufficient to drive them away from their abodes.

The following extract from "Scott's Minstrelsy of the Scottish Border" refers to the best accredited instance of the doings of the fairies that is to be found in the folklore of the north :—"It is currently believed in the north of England that he who has the courage to rush upon a fairy festival and snatch away their drinking cup, shall find it prove to him a cornucopia of good fortune if he can but bear it across a running stream."

A goblet is still preserved in Edenhall, Cumberland,

With all gay tints the darksome shade
　Grew florid as they passed along,
And not a sound their bridles made,
　But tuned itself to elfin song.

Where'er they trip, where'er they tread,
　A daisy or a bluebell springs,
And not a dewdrop shines o'erhead,
　But falls within their charmed rings.

From "Ballads by J. H. Wiffen."

which

which is supposed to have been seized at such a banquet by one of the ancient family of Musgrave.

The fairy train vanished, crying aloud :—

> If that cup ohould brcak or fall,
> Farewell the luck of Edenhall.

From this prophecy the goblet took the name it now bears : " The Luck of Edenhall."

It is worth while remarking that the two lines here put into the mouth of the fairies bear a remarkable resemblance to some of the parting shots fired off by the spaka, spamen, wizards, professors of second sight and others of the prophetic fraternity who are mentioned in the Landnama, whose communications often consist of two or more lines of poetry very abrupt in its mode of expression and couched in a form of metre or verse.

THE SPAKA* OR SEER.

The spaka, spaman, or foreteller of events is often introduced in the Landnama. His character, as described briefly, is *wise*, combined with the idea of prophetic vision or second sight.

The following passage from p. 146 will show something of the style and language of this reader of future events : " Liot rode with Guest to see him off, and asked ' What will be the cause of my death ? ' Guest said he could not definitely foretell his fate, but bade him see that he stood well with his neighbours. Liot asked : ' What ! will the earth-lice, the sons of Grim Bantling be my death then?' ' Hard bites a hungry louse,' replied Guest. ' Where will that be,' said Liot. ' Near here,' replied Guest."

" The Norwegian (Liot) rode with Guest up on to the

---

* From the same root as the Scotch and Border Spawife or fortune teller. In the old Border dialect, Spa means to foretell events.

heath

heath, and steadied Guest from behind, when his horse stumbled under him. Then said Guest: " Good luck sought thee now, but soon it must be another thing,—take care that it be not ill luck to thee."

" In that autumn Liot sat watching his slaves from a height. He had on him a cloak, the hood of which was laced round his neck, and on which there was only one sleeve. The sons of Grim Bantling rushed upon the hill and hewed at him both at once, upon which Thorkel put the hood over his head. Liot told them to behave in a neighbourly manner, and they betook themselves off from the hill by the gate along which Guest had ridden. Liot died there of his wounds. The sons of Grim went to Howard the Halt for refuge. Eyolf the Gray gave them all a reception."

This passage, I think, shows that there was evidently a firm belief in the supernatural knowledge and predictions of Guest, this prophet or wiseman, and that all he had couched in such mysterious language was looked upon as concealing or disclosing the truth.

A time there certainly was in Cumberland when such wise men or wise women were believed in and regularly consulted ; when money or other property was stolen, when cattle were ill of incurable, and apparently of inexplicable diseases, or when a man hesitated as to what course he should take in a season of doubt or uncertainty, then the wise man or wise woman was looked upon as the unerring court of final appeal. Without professing to be able to tell whence they got their information any more than I can tell where Guest got his information about Liot, I may observe that some of our Cumberland seers have at times given information and forecasts which turned out to be very near the mark. Like Guest no doubt they were thoroughly " up " in all the bearings and surroundings of the matter upon which they were consulted, and like Guest they were not by any means anxious that their
utterances

utterances should be altogether clear and to the point.*

FOLKLORE AS FOUND IN PROVERBS, PRECEPTS, AND WISE SAWS.

The short verses in which poetry and proverbs are expressed is well illustrated in the following lines, which Mr. Magnusson kindly sent to me, to show the way in which the Icelandic illustrates the meaning of our Cumberland phrase, bain way, or gain way=short cut, which corresponds almost exactly with Icelandic gayn vegr= short cut. The quotation from the Havamal, with which Mr. Magnusson explains and exemplifies this passage, is as follows :—

> Enn til gods vinar
> liggja *gagnvegir*
> pótt hann se fyrr.

Translated :—

> But to a good friend
> lie *bain ways* ever
> though he be far away.

The Havamal, from which this is quoted, is a singular collection of moral precepts and proverbs professing to be derived from Woden himself.

The poetry of Iceland consists generally of very short verses, and instead of being in rhyme it is alliterative ; that is, with two or more words in each verse or syllable commencing with the same letter. Now many of the proverbs and precepts of the Icelanders seem to partake of this alliterative character of its poetry as if they had been so formed poetically in order that they might be better remembered and handed down in the Folklore of

---

* Meg Merrilies, in Scott's Guy Mannering, represents the Border sybil or spawife, and the prophecy she gives in chapter 46 of that work is an inimitable illustration of this mysterious method of forecasting future events.

the

the people, who had to trust to their memory for all they
knew and for all they wished to refer to.

Many of these proverbs and precepts are given in
poetical form in the Landnama, and the alliteration is so
often marked, as :—

> ut heyri ek *svan sveita*
> *sara* þorns er mornar.
>
> Varat mer i *dag daudi*,
> *draugr* flatvallar baugi.
>
> Her liggr, *kjöla keyrir !*
> *Kaldakinn* um aldr.

Now, in the proverbs and wise saws to be found in the
folklore of Cumberland, this form of terse alliterative saying is often to be found exceedingly like some of the
phrases I have quoted.   Take, for example, a rhyme well
known in the folk speech long ago describing the Sundays
before Easter :—

> Tid, Mid, Missaray
> Carling, Palm, and Pace Egg Day.

This, I think, is intended to be alliterative, and three
out of the eight words which it contains are also unmistakeably Norse.

Tid is Norse for time or season ; carling comes from
cær, an accusation, and we have the very word missaray
in the Dictionary of Cleasby, where it is defined as meaning a *season* or *seasons* of the year, which definition exactly
fits it also in the lines which I have above from the Folk
Lore of our own country.

Many other similar alliterative phrases might be given :
When a man is entirely dispossessed of a home he is
said " to be turned out of *house* and *hold*," and people with
keen appetites are said to be fit to eat a man out of *house*
and *harbour*, which word *harbour*, in the sense there used,
is Norse.   Anyone who is not able to make much of a
                                                        meal

meal is said to be neither "fuller nor fainer," which word fain, or fagn, in its Cumberland form and meaning, is unmistakeably Norse. Other alliterative phrases will occur to anyone who is well acquainted with the Folk Speech and Folk Lore of Cumberland and the Lake District, such as Rig an Reean, Mack or Mell, Titter an better, and Richardson has utilised this alliterative character of our dialect in versification in a poem which he entitles "A Grummel or a Greean."

The examples given so far will, I think, be sufficient to prove that in trite saws and proverbs expressed in short words set in alliterative phrases, the two languages I am comparing have a remarkable resemblance to each other.

In Icelandic these are, I think, formed upon the model of its early poetry, of which a large portion is still extant. It is worth while remarking that with regard to the collected body of The Eddic Poems, which has been issued by the Clarendon Press, with the title of Corpus Poeticum Boreale, under the editorship of Vigfusson and Powell, the Editor Vigfusson says that * he has come to the conclusion that with one or two exceptions these poems owe their origin to Norse poets in the Western Islands ; that the lays are in fact to these Islands what the Saga was to Iceland, and that they date from a time subsequent to the settlement of Iceland from these Islands, though perhaps they are the work of the first generation after that event. In the Western Islands† as here named he includes Great Britain (the Northern portion, including North English Counties), Ireland, Man, the Hebrides, and the Orkneys. He shows from internal evidence of place-names and references that some of the poems were most probably composed there. Wherever they may have been written

---

* See Prolegomena to Sturlunga Saga, vol. I., p. 186.
† Throughout the Landnama two divisions of Icelandic Settlers are noted, viz.: Eastmen, or those who came from Norway ; and Westmen, or those who came from the British or Western Islands.

these

these poems are very largely employed in describing the
Northern mythology, or like the Havamal, used for teaching moral precepts and inculcating proverbs and trite
home truths.

There is a very forcible passage in the Havamal which
gives a good idea of the Icelandic, or as it may be put of
the Northern poetry and of the style of alliterative expression.

Sir G. Desant applies this passage to Cleasby and to his
arduous labours in the language, and with it I may con-
clude this paper.   It is as follows :—

> Deyr fe' Deyja fraendr,
> Deyjr Sjalfr it sama,
> En ord.stirr deyr aldregi
> Hveim ser godan getr.

I have translated it and attempted to retain some of its
alliterative force :—

> Dies wealth,¦die friends,
>   Yourself shall die ;
> If rich or poor, 'tis all the same,
> Virtue alone can reach the sky,
> The glory of a God-got name.

Glossary of Fell, Field, and Farm Names closely allied or identical in Lakeland or Iceland.

THE Book of the Icelandic settlement is essentially a book of place names. The places of which the names are given and recorded are the hills, dales, fields, and farms that marked the claims of the early settlers. A careful study of the Landnama will convince the student that the Norse system of name giving was looked upon as a religious ceremony.

In the case of men's names this is obvious enough. The head of the clan or family was both priest and chief. When consecrated to the priesthood, as priest (Godi) he took the name of Thor or the Divinity in addition to his own name. Hence men who were originally called Rolf, Steinn or Stone, and Grim, on being dedicated to the priesthood became Thorolf, Thorsteinn,* and Thorgrim, and hence in the Register of men's names found in the Landnama Book are no less than sixteen pages of men's names commencing with Thor, which is more than one-fifth of the whole list.

In the same manner the assigning of place names was in some measure a consecration of the land to the use of the settler and to the care of the Divinity.

The following passage, which I have translated from p. 234 of the Landnama, will show what I mean :—" Two brothers came from the Orkneys and sailed to the North and West of Iceland. They struck in an Ax at Reistarg-nap and called it Oxarfjord=Axfrith: they placed an eagle to the west and called the place Arnarthufu or Eagle's Mound ; in a third place they reared a cross, and

---

* Thirlmere is said to have been originally Thorolfsmere, and as I have noted elsewhere Thurston or Thorsteinn water was the original name of Coniston Lake.

called

called the place Crossas, or Crosswater, and so they hallowed for themselves or consecrated the whole of Oxarford." It is not difficult in Lakeland to mention names almost exactly similar to the names here given, such as Oxenfell, Crosscrake, and Arnside.

And, as in the present instance, also elsewhere many settlers were passing and repassing to and from the British Islands, we may safely assume that a similar process of name-giving took place upon our northern shores, and when we find, as we often do find, names closely allied or identical in Lakeland, and Iceland it is very strong evidence that they were assigned under like conditions, and where Ari assigns a reason and a derivation for it in the Icelandic Landtake we may assume a similar reason and a similar derivation in the North English Landtake as well. This principle has guided me in the selection of place names that I have made in the following Glossary, and as will be seen they are chiefly names applied to the farms and homesteads or used in the apportioning of claims or settlements of land.

GLOSSARY,

ARN or ORN, *an eagle.* ARNARHVAL, eagle's knoll. Compare Arnside: see remarks under " side " in this Glossary.

BIRK, *The Birch*, Birker, The Birks, Birks Bridge, as surname Birkett.

BRANDRITH, *a grate*, both in Lakeland and Iceland. In Lakeland originally an iron tripod held together by rims of iron and employed in supporting the girdle plate which was used above the hearth fire for baking oat bread. The three Shire stones near the source of the Duddon were called "The Three-legged Brandrith," because a person might there at the same time place each of his feet in a separate county, Cumberland and Westmorland, and his hands in a third county, Lancashire, thus forming a kind of living brandrith.

The name Brandrith is also applied to the point where the boundaries of three parishes meet. For a somewhat similar reason a mountain near the Great Gable is called "The Brandrith," and where the rivers Brathay and. Rothay meet at their confluence with the Lake of Windermere; the place is called "The Brandrith" the two rivers and the Lake forming as it were the legs.

BRANDRITH STONE: A boundary stone at the meeting of three parishes.

BY: The origin of this name has been discussed at p. 18. By, is very common throughout Scandinavia; and in the north and east of England the Bys are unnumbered; wherever the Scandinavian tribes went bu or bö or by went with them. Kirkby= Kirkjabaer in Iceland. It has been shown elsewhere that baer, bae, bu, and by, are only inflexional variations of this word. Scotby is Scotman's bu, or dwelling, and Ireby is Irishman's bu. In Scale*by*, or bu, we have a place name identical with Scale bu, otherwise Scale toft, which describes the settlement of one of the original settlers of Iceland.

CARR: Applied as the name of fields and woods which in the Lake District are sometimes known as " The Carrs ". In Cumberland small cup-shaped fields surrounded by Alders or Ellers are called

called Ellercars. Carr corresponds, says Magnusson, to Danish Kaer; Ice. Kjarr and Norw. Kjerr, all indicative of straggling wood growing in marshy places, or of mossy tracts more or less under water.

CINDER, Ice. SINDR, *slag* or *dróss* : This word is applied to the slag or dross containing a large percentage of iron which is found on the margin of Wastwater and Coniston and other lakes, also in the Duddon valley. It indicates the sites of the Old Blooma-ries, where the iron was brought to be smelted; suppressed in the Coniston and Hawkshead district in A.D. 1565, the 7th year of Queen Elizabeth, the tenants agreeing amongst themselves, to pay an annual rent of £20, called Bloomsmithy rent. Many field names, &c., are derived from it; *e.g.*, Cinder Hill, Cinder How, Cinder Nab, Cinder Beck, Cinder Barrow.

COMBE or KAMB: I take these words to have been originally the same, though now they are distinct in the Lake District. Combe is the ridge of a hill, as Black Combe; Kam is the ridge or pointed top of a fence wall. A serrated and pointed top is termed a Yorkshire Cam. Catcam on Helvellyn implies a cam so steep as would turn a cat. Very frequent in Icelandic place names of crags rising like a crest; originally a crest or comb. Ladies used to wear costly combs of walrus tusk; hence the place where Queen Aud lost her comb overboard is called Kambness.—Landnama, III.

CROSS; Ice. KROSS : The rearing of crosses and consequent cross worship as mentioned in the account of Queen Aud, at p. xv, seems to have been the origin in Iceland of many place names commencing in Cross. Cross Fell, Cumberland, is said to take its name from a Cross, having been reared there to exorcise demons. The rushing of Helm winds and other "uncanny" noises having secured for it the name and reputation of Fiends' Fell before this.

COTE ; Ice. COT : A cottage or small farmhouse. This word is often found as the name of places bordering on the Solway. In the Abbey Holme, for example, are these farms : The Cote, Seaville Cote, Raby Cote, Skinburness Cote, East Cote; also Sea Cote, and a Cumberland Parish is named Cote Hill.

DEEAL or DALE (Norse, DEILA, *to divide*); a division or share as of a town or common field which, though unenclosed, had its pro-duce divided or parcelled out into separate portions, the owner-ship of which changed annually in succession. O.E.: Deal or divide. Romans : According as God hath *dealt* to every man.

DEEAL

DEEAL or DALE : *A dale or valley.*   The Icelandic Dalr, a *valley*, cor-corresponds exactly in meaning and application with this word dale or deeal as found in Lakeland as place-name.   As place names they have a similar application in the following :—

In Iceland.		In Lakeland.
Thver-dalr	*corresponds with*	Cross dale.
Djupi-dalr	,,	Deep dale.
Breid-dalr	,,	Broad dale.
Langi-dalr	,,	Lang dale.
Fagri dalr	,,	Fair dale.

The term "dalesmen" is applied to mountaineers in both countries.

DILLICAR : From Carr, as above, and daela, *a dell-shaped sink or scoop in the ground* ; a name generally applied to small, scoop-shaped fields in Lakeland.   There is an instance in this parish where six such fields, together forming something like a circle, are called Dillicars.

ELLER (*the alder tree*), Dan. ELLER : Elterwater, Langdale, a tarn, so called from the alders which grow on its margin.   "The Ellers," Ulverston ; Ellercar in North England and Denmark applied to small cup-shaped meadows surrounded by alder trees.

FELL : *A mountain.*   The Icelandic form is Fjall ; Norwegian, Fjeld, pronounced Fiell.   In the Lake District it is applied to particular mountains, as Scawfell, Kirkfell, Bowfell.   Also applied to a mountain district generally which is termed the Fell.   The unenclosed upland common is also called the Fell, as in the following verse from Richardson :—

> Ya winter neet, aw meynd it weel,
> Our fowk hed been at Fell ;
> An beein tired went suin ta bed,
> An aw sat be mesel.

FRITH ; Ice. FJORD : *A frith or bay.*   Milli fjell ok fjordr, *between the fell and the frith,* is a favourite alliterative phrase for describing settlements in the Landnama.   The fjordr, which was larger than the Vik or Creek, corresponds exactly in name and meaning with Frith, as found in the North of England and Scotland.   In an old list of the Friths in the West and North of Iceland, about one hundred such Friths are given, generally prefixed with names describing either their physical characteristics or some incident connected with the settlement.   In Iceland shore districts are divided into Friths, just as mountain districts are
divided

divided into Dales. Hence it is extensively used as a place name, and the Eastern and Western parts of Iceland are called the vest firdir and aust firdir, *i.e.*, the west and east Friths.

FLOW; Ice. FLOI: *An expanse of marshy waste*, as Wedholme Flow, Bowness Flow, Flow Moss (near Shap), Floutern Tarn. In Icelandic Floi is a marsh mossy waste, hence applied to a district in the south of that Island. Flugumyri, the name of a well-known farm. The Burning of Flugumyri, to which it gives the name, is one of the most tragic events in the History of the Commonwealth, as the inhabitants were fought back and imprisoned within their home while it was being burned over their heads.

GAP; Ice. GAP: an opening or pass between mountains, as Scarf Gap, Raise Gap, Whinlatter Gap. Gap in dialect is an opening or gap in fences.

GARTH and GARDS: These words appear as Gardr in Icelandic, and Gard in the Bible of Ulphilas, where sheepfold as it occurs in John x, is translated Gards. The words signify anything which is *girt*, or *enclosed, an enclosed space*. They often occur in place-names, as The Gards, Grass-gards, Mell-gards, Garth Nook, Dale-garth. In some parts of Cumberland the garden in the dialect was always " the garth "; also Stackgard was Stackgarth; Churchyard, Kurkgarth.

GEIT, a *goat*, Norse; occurs as part of place-name in Landnama; often used as place-name in Lakeland, as Gatesgill, Gatesgarth, Gateswater, Gatescale, Gatescarth.

GILL: a ravine, generally with a rush of water through it, as Dungeon Gill, Gill Spout, Stockgill, Stanley Gill containing Dalegarth Force, corresponds with Icelandic Gil, a deep narrow ravine with a stream at the bottom; if there be no stream the term Gill is not used. In Iceland are places called Gill Banks, Hell Gill, *i.e.*, *Covered* Gill; often as farm or place-name as The Gill, Aigle Gill, Gillerthwaite, Ashgill, Ivegill, How Gill, Gill Foot, Gill Head; Horse Gills, Yearn Gill, Hugill, Gilsland, Hethersgill.

GRISE (Norse: Gris, a Swine): Grisedale, Grisedale Tarn, Grisebeck, possibly also Grassmere or Gricemere; confer Swindale and Swinside from Swine.

GRUND, Ice.: *A grassy field or plain*; the name of a farm in Landnama, which would thus literally be *green field*. This name is often referred to in the Sturlunga Saga as the residence of two

men

men who take great part in Icelandic history.   In Iceland it has evidently been applied first to single fields, then to farms of which these fields formed a part.   GRUND, as farm name, occurs very frequently in Furness, and most likely originated in the same way.   The name is now often written " ground," but the original form and dialect pronunciation is GRUND, as Sandgrund, or ground.   Sawrey Grund, Holm Grund, Brocklebank Grund, Park Grund.   H. Swainson-Cowper, F.S.A., kindly collected for me the names of this class.   In Furness alone he enumerated forty-seven grunds, or grounds, generally joined with personal names.

HELM, *a covering*: From the Norse HJALMR, A.S., Eng. and Ger. HELM; derived from Icelandic hylja, *to hide.*   In this acceptation it is given by Vigfusson as applied in popular tales to the cap of darkness, which makes the wearer invisible, and so it is applied in the Norse to the clouds as rendering the mountains invisible. There are several mountains called Helm in Iceland and in Norway; and we have it applied in the same sense in Lakeland to the Helm cragg; it is also used as a surname.   It is from the original sense of covering or hiding that we get the name Helm in Helm Winds ; for Helm is the name of the cap or covering of clouds which descends upon the summits of Cross Fell at the time when the Helm wind blows.

HOLM ; from Ice. HOLMR : *An island, especially in a lake or creek, also of low land near a river or lake.*   This corresponds exactly with its meaning in the Lake District.   There are the following Holms, on Windermere : Rough Holm, Lady Holm, Hen Holm, House Holm, Thompson's Holm, Ramp Holm, Ling Holm, Grass Holm, Silver Holm, Blake Holm,—these are mostly is- lands.   It is also applied to lowlying land near the sea or a river, as Abbey Holme, Holm Eden, Willow Holm.
The Norse Thing was generally assembled near or upon a Holm or Island, and the Holmgang or Final Court of Appeal by Battle takes its name from having been fought upon a Holm or Island. An Island or Holm is still pointed out in the Shetlands, ap- proached by stepping stones, where the Thing assembled, which in name, constitution, and all that concerned it, seems to have been essentially Norse.

How: Originally *a grave mound*; then a gentle eminence or mound, frequent in proper names.   Used in this sense of Silver How, Fox How, Torpenhow (compare Hill of Howth, near Dublin). Howie is still used as grave mound in the Shetlands, according
to

to Edmoston. Queen Aud's mound, under the name of How or
Haugr, was regarded with veneration by her descendants under
the impression that they should *die into it*; that is, live in it after
death. There are the following place-names with How in Cum-
berland and Westmorland, and some of them have been shown
by actual examination to be graves, presumably those of Norse-
men:—Black How, Brown How, Bull How, Bought How,
Broad How, Cinder How, Corn How, Cropple How, Flake How,
Gunner's How, Hund How, Kemp How, Kitts How, Lamb How,
Otts How, Red How, Scout How, Silver How, Soulby How,
Scale How, Tanner How, Thorney How, Whelp How, Wads
How.

HUMMER: In Lakeland *a grassy slope by the side of a river.*
"Hummers dark," a phrase that occurs in Gibson's "Folk
Speech." Ice. HVAMMR or HVAMMA=*a grassy slope or vale.*
Vigfusson says it is very frequent as an appellation in every
Icelandic farm. It also means a swamp, and is in this sense
applied in Lakeland as name of wet land.

The word illustrates the varied history of the same word in different countries. While in Lakeland it has become an obscure
and almost obsolete word in the dialect, or a place name hardly
recognised, in Iceland as HVAMMA or HVAM, the name of the
home of the noble and talented family of the Sturlungs, it is one
of the most memorable and renowned place-names in the history
of the Icelandic Commonwealth.

KELD, *a well or spring*, Ice. KELD, Dan. KELDE, a well or spring :
in place-names as Threlkeld, Iron Keld, Butterilket=Butterild
Keld and Keldrü, a well, with a stream or a flowing from it.

KNOTT, *a rocky excrescence* generally proceeding from the top of
a mountain, Ice. KNUTA: frequently, as Magnusson explains,
applied to the tops of mountains in eastern Iceland, which re-
semble the knob of the "femur" which moves in the socket of
the hip bone. This word as applied to mountains is of frequent
use as a place-name in Lakeland, as Knott End, Benson Knott,
Knott Rigg, Hard Knott=Harte Knott or Hard Knott in Norway
where many other corresponding place-names in Knott are found.

KNAB, *a rocky promontory*, Ice. KNAPPR, a nob or button-shaped
peak : examples of place-names—The Knab, Nab End, Knapping
Tree=Nab end Tree.

KIRK=KIRKJA in Iceland, KIRK in Scotland, and KIRKE in Denmark,
a church. There is a mountain called Kirkfell in Wasdale
Head

Head—so called doubtless because the mountain church there stands not far from it. There is a Kirkfell in Iceland also, and the Frith on which it stands is called Kirkjufjordr or Kirkfrith; Kirkju-baer in Iceland corresponds exactly with Kirkby in the North of England; about 20 or 30 such names are found in maps of northern England marking churches built by the Danish or Norse settlers. There are the following parishes commencing with Kirk in this diocese:—Kirkby Kendal, Kirkandrews (2), Kirkbampton, Kirkbride, Kirkby Ireleth, Kirkby Lonsdale, Kirkby Stephen, Kirkby Thore, Kirkland, Kirklinton, Kirkoswald. Kirk is also found as parish and church-name in the Isle of Man. Kirk or Kurk was the name for church used in the Cumberland dialect, *e.g.*, Kurkgarth=Churchyard, Ice. Kirkju-gards. The introduction of Christianity into Iceland and with it the use of the word Kirkju, is described in chapter 49 of the Erybjgga Saga, A.D. 1000. A curious legend, for the purpose of encouraging men to build churches, is told in that chapter where it is said that a man could grant as many souls a seat in Heaven as the church he built held persons.

LATH, a barn, O.N. KLATHA, Dan. LAD: Leathes, a village in Cumberland; Watendlath=Barn at the end of the Wath; and Silloth =Sellath, may all be from this root. Ireleth is Irishman's barn, as Ireby is Irishman's "bu," or dwelling.

LUND=*a grove or wood* : in Iceland originally a sacred wood, or grove dedicated to a God, as in the following passage at p. 224 of Landnama :—"Thorir dwelt at Lund=the Grove, and worshipped the Grove or Lund." It occurs in Lake District as place-name, also as surname.

MIRE; Ice. MYRR: In both applied to boggy or swampy ground, and in both frequently used as place-name, as The Mires, Mire Side, Pelutho Mire, Mire House. We have also as surname Myers, Mirehouse. Myra is the name of a County in Iceland and men from that County are called Myramenn.

MEER STONES, a word allied to the foregoing. In Lakeland stones placed at the boundaries of undivided allotments to mark the limits of the owners. Many of the old allotments were thus divided, and there are still stones so standing and so named. There were undivided portions of land, so situated, and stones so placed in this parish (Torver) to mark three adjoining ownerships. They existed until the year before last, when the whole three portions having fallen into one ownership, the stones lost their significance as land marks. Seems to correspond exactly with

with the Lyritr of Iceland which is explained in this way:—
"When the boundary of a field or estate was to be drawn, the
law prescribed that a mark stone (marksteinn) should be raised
upon the spot and three other stones laid beside it, called land
mark stones, and by their number and position they were distinguished from all other stones in the field."

MEOL (*Sandhills*): A Norse word, so called from the meal-like ap-
pearance of the sand, *e.g.*, Esk Meals, Mealsgate, Cartmel,
Millom. The way in which this word was applied in the original
settlement of Iceland is related in a curious story, at p. 76 of
the Landnama. An original settler was told that his son should
take land where his mare should lay down under a cliff. The
mare went before them until she came to two red sandhills
(sand mēlir treir raudir); she then lay down under the cliff of a
sandhill (mēlir), and he took up his abode there, and called the
place Raudamel or Rauda meol, *i.e.*, the red sand hills.

RAKE : In the Lake Country is applied generally to the narrow path
along which sheep *are driven* to the fell. It is used in the same
acceptation in Yorkshire from the verb reka, past rūk, originally
vrēka=*to drive*, "Outrake" corresponding in sense and sound with
the Norse ùt reka was a path by which sheep were *driven out* to
the fell. There is one so named on Black Combe, one at Torver,
one at Coniston ; there seems to be one or more in most of the
larger valleys in Lakeland, which were spoken of as "The
Rake," just as we speak of "The Fell." There are also several
farms in the district called "The Outrake," and I have observed
that such farms generally stand at the entrance to a Rake or
Fell drive. The Norse verb vreka also means to drive or drift
as the tide does, and we have this in the place-name of Wreaks
End, near Broughton-in-Furness, which takes its name from a
point in the stream close by, which marks the end of the tide-
flow or drift. On Yorkshire moors sheep are said *to rake out*
when they are driven single file.

REEAN (in Furness); REIN or RANE (in Cumberland and Westmorland): The Reeans in Furness were unploughed portions which
were left round cultivated fields known in other parts of the
country as Head Riggs. The origin of the name seems, however, to have been from the cultivated strips which, before
town, fields, and commons were divided by fences, were left
untilled in order to mark the boundaries. Some of the older inhabitants remember perfectly when this system was in use here.
The same system was known also in Westmorland, for J. B.
Davies

Davies, Esq., of Kirkby Stephen, says:—"The name 'reins' is also used here for narrow strips of land, a little higher than the ground on either side, left in closes called field lands or dale lands to mark the division of such land or dale. We have fields called Raynes, sloping lands with riggs or terraces, on the lower side of which is usually a reean, or slightly elevated strip. These slightly elevated strips have often been levelled down, but the name is still retained." The same system prevailed in Cumberland, and Dickinson in his Glossary of the Cumberland Dialect (English Dialect Society) defines Rig and Rane as "an arable field held in shares which are divided by narrow green lanes (ranes) and the intervals usually cultivated." The system formerly prevailed in Yorkshire.

ROWANTREE: *The mountain ash*; Ice. REGNIR, Dan. RONNETREE. This word marks very clearly the connexion between the words and superstitions of Iceland and of the North of England. The Rowan tree was a holy tree consecrated to Thor, and according to the legends quoted by Magnusson very intimately connected with the mysteries and superstitions of the Icelanders. It was thus it was used to mark place names at the time of the settlement as the only sort of tree except the dwarf birch that was found in Iceland. In some places in the North of England a piece of the Rowan tree was placed above the door to scare away evil influences, and in Lakeland the stick for stirring the cream was frequently of Rowan tree wood to counteract the influence that bewitched the churn so that no butter was forthcoming. In Yorkshire a piece of Rowan tree wood was carried for security against witches, and called witch wood.

RIVER NAMES: Rivers or streams are often mentioned in Landnama as bounding a Landtake, and one settler is spoken of as making a fire at every river mouth that defined his Landtake. A=a river occurs in Hita=a hot river being formed from a hot spring as distinguished from Kalda, or cold river. These two names are brought into juxta position at p. 74 of the Landnama, where it is said of a settler he took land between the hot river and the cold river, Hita ok Kalda. Laxa is the salmon river. A=river is found as termination of many of our local rivers, as Rotha, Bratha, Greta, Wisa and Kalda. The *meeting of rivers* is in Icelandic termed *A*mot, and we have a corresponding word in Eamont, formerly spelled Amont and Amot.

RUD or RJODR, *a clearing* (see p. 18, where the settlement of Steinolf is described). We have the word as a dialect word, at any rate

in

in High Furness, where to *rud* or *rid* a wood means to *clear it,*—
that is to clear it out root and branch. Riddins, or Riddings, as
place name is used in the same acceptation. I think in this
word we retain a trace of *inn* the Norse suffixed article.

SAND : As field and farm name occurs often in Cumberland and
other parts of Lakeland, as Sandside, Sandgap, Sandlands,
Sandscale, Sandraw, Sandwith, Sandal, Sandsfield. The Landnama, or its accompanying map, gives the following place
names in Iceland : Sanda, Sandfell, Sandbrekka, Sand dalr,
Sand eyrr, Sandgil, Sandholar, Sandvik ; Sand has the same
meaning in both cases.

SEL : *An Icelandic word very frequent in Landnama,* meaning *a shed
on a mountain pasture* but within the landmarks of each farm,
where the milk cows were kept in summer. These sels origin-
ate the following place names which are found in Landnama
with this meaning : Sel, Selja, Selja land, Sel-tungur, Sel hagi,
Sela, Sel dalr, Sel heidr. We certainly have it as a portion of
place names in Lakeland and its district, as Sella, Sellafield,
Sylecroft, Selside, Silloth.

SET : *a seat or settlement,* is found in the Icelandic place-name, SET-
BERG, the *mountain seat* from the idea of fairies having their
seat or abode upon the mountain ; compare Sedbergh, Satterthwaite, &c.

SIDE appears, says Ferguson, to be used in the sense of settlement, Norse Sida ; *e.g.,* Ayside, Ambleside, Arnside, Kettleside,
Ormside, Swinside, Selside. Ferguson, in accordance with the
system laid down in another part of his valuable and learned
work, takes these words to be from side=a settlement, coupled
with Hamil, Arni, Ketil, Ornir, Svein. With regard to Arn,
otherwise Orn, it is frequently used in Landnama, as a place
name ; generally, however, it is derived from Arn=an eagle
(see passage from Landnama quoted at the introduction to
this Glossary), and not from a man's name, as Ferguson says.
Ayside : I take it to be from A a *stream* and side=the settlement
by the stream.

SCALE : *A shelter or hut,* as Scales, Seascale, Scale Hill, Sandscale,
Bowscale. Another form of the word as found upon the Border
is Shields, as Winter Shields, Shield Green, Hole Shields. In
this form we have the word shieling, or hut. We have Scale in
the dialect of Lakeland as a common noun, as Peat Scale.
There is a remarkable confirmation of this use of the word in
The

the Landnama, at p. 35, where it is said of Leif, who came from the British Islands with Ingolf, his foster brother, the original settler, that "he made two Scala or Scales" for shelter, and this word is explained in the Icelandic as meaning a square piece of ground with walls but without roof. Portingscale=Porthing-scale may contain within it the word Thing, compounded with Scala the huts or booths erected as temporary dwellings when men were attending the Thing.

SOWERBY, Ice. SAURBAE : The origin of this place name has been discussed at p. 18. There are three districts of this name mentioned in Landnama, and more appear in an old map of Iceland.

STED, *a place or sted.* The use of this word as farm name is very common in the Landnama. We have it often also as suffix in farm names in High Furness.

SWIN, *a swine.* There are Swindales both in Lakeland and Iceland (for the origin of the latter see p. 25). I think this derivation may afford the key to the derivation of other local place names commencing with Swin, as Swinside, Swinsty.

TOFT, *a homestead* ; the farm house including the farm buildings ; a word in very general use in Cumberland. In a Court Book of the manor of Derwentwater is the record that Gawen Wren was fined ten shillings about the year 1640 for having two fires in one *toft* at the same time. At p. 35 of the Landnama it is recorded of Leif, the companion of Ingolf, that when he first landed he built two Tofts, one eighteen fathoms long and the other nineteen, and he resided in them the first winter. In Cumberland Toft was so much used as common noun for the name of farm buildings that it is nowhere found as proper noun or place name, and I cannot understand how Taylor says, as he does, at p. 115 of his " Words and Places," that in the Lake District " Toft " is unknown. Will he tell us any name for farm buildings that was better known ?

THOR : As a place name occurs in Thursby, where it is recorded was a temple to Thor, whose supposed foundations were dug up about the end of last century. Thurston (Thorsteinn) Water, the ancient name of Coniston Lake, Thurston Ville, and Thurstonfield. Thor, as the name of their Chief Divinity, enters more largely into the nomenclature of the early Norsemen than any other word (see introduction to this Glossary).

TON, TOUN, or TUN, *a field*, then *a farm.* Upon both the Cumbrian and

and the Scottish side of the Border tùn is applied to a single farm house with its outbuildings, &c. Originally this word meant a field surrounded by a hedge, and in this sense Wycliffe translates Matt. xxii., 5 : "But thei dispiseden, and wenten forth—one into his toun (field), another to his merchandise."
In the Waverley of Sir Walter Scott, toun or tùn is applied to a single farm upon the Border : " He hes dune neathing but dance up an' doun the toun." This application might be indefinitely extended upon the Border, where every farm is called a toun or tùn, and Whamtùn, Uppertoun, and Bartiestoun, are either single farm houses or hamlets with three or four farm houses. Low-thertoun, Longtoun, are larger villages, but still from the same derivation, and so on with the other tons of the county.

TUN corresponds with the Icelandic tùn, properly a hedge, then a hedged or fenced plot within which a house is built, then the farmstead with its buildings=the homestead. In Norse deeds each single farm is called a tun, and the Icelandic phrase, tùn fra tùni, means from house to house. The ancient Scandinavians, like the other old Teutonic peoples, had no towns. Tacitus says :—" Nullas Germanorum populis urbes habitari, satis notum est ; ne pati quidem junctas sedes. Colunt discreti, ac diversi, ut, fons, ut campus, ut nemus placuit." And with regard to Iceland those words of Tacitus " colunt discreti ac diversi," still apply, for excepting the Capital, which is but a village, all the other so-called tùns are single farms.

THWAITE : *A piece of land cut off by a fence or enclosed* ; also as a cutting or clearing. ICE. THVEIT=cut-off piece. Thwaites were originally fenced or cut off, and in this sense the word is still used as a field name in High Furness. From being a field name thwaite gradually became applied to farms and then to villages and parishes. In this sense it occurs more than one hundred times in Cumberland alone. It is also found in High Furness as surname. In Norway and Lakeland the following names are almost exactly alike in form and meaning :—

Lakeland.			*Norway.*
The Thwaite	.....	.... .	Thveit
Applethwaite	.....	....	Epelthwait
Birkthwaite	.....	....	Birkethvet
Birthwaite	.....	.....	Barthwet
Branthwaite) Braithwaite)	.....	.....	Brandsthvet
Micklethwaite	....	.....	Mykelthvet
			Seathwaite

Lakeland,			Norway.
Seathwaite	.....	.....	Sjothvet
Ruthwaite	....	.....	Rugthvet

THING, Ice.: *An assembly or meeting, a Parliament including law courts*:—

1 United Parliament in Iceland was called Althing.*
2 Thing founded by Thorolf at Thorsness was Quarter Thing, or County Thing, or Council.
3 A Parish was also called Thing.

The date of the Althing being formed in Iceland from Norway is given in Landnama as in A.D. 927. Hacon, son of Harald Fairhaired, was the first Founder of the Norwegian Constitution, and of its political division into Things. Vigfusson quotes a passage to this effect from Heimskringla. Do we retain in our place names any evidence of this institution of Thing? Addingham and Aldingham are suggested as from Althing.

ULPH or ULF=WOLF: *Much used in the Norse, as personal and place names.* Compare Ulverston, Ulpha, Ullswater, Lyulphs Tower near Ullswater, Ulphilas, the name of Moeso Gothic Bishop is the diminutive form of the word=little wolf.

With regard to Ulverston, its origin and meaning as a place name has been much discussed. About 25 years ago there was a keen controversy in the local papers as to whether it should be Ulverston or Ulverstone, ton being the spelling of those who took it from tun or ton as discussed in this Glossary and the supporters of stone instanced a large *stone* from which the name was said to be derived, amongst the latter were the authorities of the Union by whom the spelling Ulverstone was retained for many years.

ULVERSTON is derived by Taylor (Names & Places, p. 116), from Olafr, a Christian name. Most of those place names, however, were probably given before men had christian names of all. I think Ulverston comes from Ulphr or Ulfr. The settlement of a man named Ulfr is described at page 63 of the Landnama. Take this with tun or ton and the Icelandic derivation becomes obvious enough. Ulfr's descendants and their Landtake are also noted at page 63 of the Landnama, and one of them settled at Lundi,

* The Althing still exists in Iceland ; consists of thirty-six members, thirty of whom are elected by household suffrage and six nominated by the King of Denmark. Sits in two divisions, twelve members in upper division and twenty-four in lower.

or The Lund.* I think it is worth while remarking in this connexion that of the twenty-four parishes or ratepaying districts or townships included in the Ulverston Union the following names are Icelandic or Norse :—

Aldingham, Allithwaite, Angerton. Cartmel Fell, Claife, Dalton, Dunnerdale with Seathwaite, Hawkshead, Skelwith, Kirkby Ireleth, Lowick and Subberthwaite, Satterthwaite, Ulverston, Urswick.

With regard to Angerton—the same as place-name occurs on the coast of the Solway in the Abbey Holme, and there is an Icelandic place-name given in the Landnama exceedingly like it. Claife means, I think, the hill or cliff, and as such is represented in sense and sound in Icelandic. Hawk, or Hauk, is a surname in the Landnama, and one of its earliest editions is called Hauksbook, from Hauk, the name of its editor. Head in Hawkshead comes I think from a corresponding Norse word meaning a hill or hill rise—such a hill is near Hawkshead Church and the Churchyard is situated partly upon it.

WYKE or WICK or VIK, Norse: *A creek or bay*, as Pull Wyke Bay, or Pool Wyke on Windermere, Pull Wyke on Bassenthwaite, Sandwick on Ulleswater. The old Norse rovers were called Vikings or Creekers from frequenting creeks or bays. There is a small opening or sea creek called Fleswick, situated between the north head and south head of St. Bees, a pretty and retired spot which Gibson in one of his folk speech songs notes as the western terminus of Cumberland. There is a Fleswick upon the opposite coast of the Isle of Man ; these identical names show, I think, that there was a corresponding settlement on the Manx and the Cumbrian coast.

---

* The Icelandic Ulfr had a Lund=Grove near his settlement and the North English Ulfr seems to have had a Lund near his settlement too.

LIST· OF SUBSCRIBERS.

Ayre, Rev. L. R., R.D., Holy Trinity Vicarage, Ulverston.
Adams, J. R., Esq., 66, Cannon Street, London.
Atkinson, James, Esq., King Street, Ulverston.
Atkinson, H., Esq., 20, North Road, Birkenhead (2 copies).
Ainsworth, Col., J.P., D.L., Broughton Hall, Grange-over-Sands,
Ashburner, Rev. John, The Vicarage, Blawith.
Alcock-Beck, W., Esthwaite Lodge, Hawkshead, Ambleside.

Barrow-in-Furness, The Bishop of, The Abbey, Carlisle.
Barrow-in-Furness Free Library.
Bell, John, Esq., Hawsbank, Coniston (2 copies).
Butler, J. R., Esq., Broughton-in-Furness (2 copies).
Brockbank, Mrs., The Croft, Kirksanton.
Baldwin, Colonel, J.P., Dalton-in-Furness.
Bibliothica Jacksonia, Tullie House, Carlisle.
Billinge, Rev. R. B., Urswick Vicarage, Ulverston.
Bland, Miss, Shap Wells Hotel, Shap.
Bower, Rev. R., Vicar of St. Cuthbert's, Carlisle.
Beardsley Dr., Grange-over-Sands (3 copies).
Barratt, J. W. H., Esq., J.P., Holywath, Coniston.
Barratt, W. I., Esq., J.P., Broom Hill, Broughton-in-Furness.
Benn T., Esq., Bankfield, Millom.
Benson, T. Esq., Stable Harvey, Torver.
Bell, William, Esq., J.P., Haws Bank, Coniston.
Barrow, William, Esq., Gateside, Coniston.

Campbell, Rev. H. E., St. George's Vicarage, Millom.
Crewdson, W. D., Esq., Helm Lodge, Kendal.
Collingwood, W. G. Esq., M.A., Lane Head, Coniston.
Conder, E., Esq., New Court, Colwall, Herefordshire.
Calverley, Rev. W. S., F.S.A., Aspatria Vicarage, Carlisle.
Cross, Viscount, G.C.B., Eccle Riggs, Broughton-in-Furness (2 copies)
Coward, J., Esq., Fountain Street, Ulverston.

Dunn, J. M., Esq., 30, Claverton Street, Pimlico, London.
Dawe, Rev. W. P., Satterthwaite Vicarage, Ulverston.
Dickinson, Rev. W. T., Frodsham, Cheshire.
Dunn, Miss, 30, Claverton Street, Pimlico, London.

Ellwood, Rev. T. E., 4, Byron Street, Patricroft, Manchester (2 copies).

Ellwood, J. F. A. Esq., Mail s.s. Strabo.
Ecroyd, W., Esq., Lomeshaye, Nelson.
Ellwood, G. B., Esq.. Barrow-in-Furness.
Ellwood, R. D., Esq., Torver Rectory, Coniston, Lancashire.

Fawcitt, Dr., Broughton-in-Furness (3 copies).
Ferguson, The Worshipful Chancellor, F.S.A., Carlisle.
Ferguson, Robert, Esq., Beach House, The Mall, Hammersmith W.
    (2 copies).
Fell, Dr., T. K., 6, Harley Street, Barrow-in-Furness.
Fell, John, Esq., J.P. & D.L., Flan How, Ulverston.
Firth, Rev. William W. D., The Vicarage, Patricroft, Manchester.

Garner, John, Esq., The Garner, Broughton-in-Furness.
Glaister, T., Esq., Saltcoats, Abbey Town, Carlisle.

Haines, C. S., Esq., Beech Grove, Ulverston.
Herford, Rev. R. Travers, Stand Parsonage, Manchester.
Hope, Rev. R. D., Old Hutton Vicarage, Kendal.
Hibbert, P., Esq., Plumtree Hall, Milnthorpe.
Harry, J. H., Esq., High Laws House.
Hoare, Rev. J. W., F.R.Hist.S., St. John's Vicarage, Keswick.
Hodgson, James, Esq., J.P., Britain Place, Ulverston (2 copies).
Holme, James, Esq., Blake Holme, Newby Bridge, Ulverston.

Jones, F. M. T., Esq., Lesketh How, Ambleside (2 copies).

Kewley, Rev. W., The Vicarage, Ulpha, Broughton-in-Furness.
Kenworthy, Rev. J. W., Vicar of Braintree, Essex.

Laverty, Rev. P., Presbytery, Coniston.
Lowthian, Rev. W., Troutbeck, Windermere.
Lund, J., Esq., Torver, Coniston.
Lowry, Rev. C. H., The Vicarage, Kirkby Ireleth.

Magnusson, E., Esq., M.A., University Library, Cambridge (2 copies).
Marshall, S. A., Esq., J.P., Skelwith Fold, Ambleside (2 copies).
Mayhew, Rev. A. L., Treasurer of English Dialect Society, Brad-
    more Road, Oxford.
Metcalfe, W., Esq., 33, Chiswick Street, Carlisle.
Millom Free Public Library.
Micklethwaite, J. T., Esq., F.S.A., 15, Dean's Yard, Westminster.
Moser, G. E., Esq., Kendal.
Mechanics Institute, Coniston.

Nicholson, J. H., Esq., M.A., Whitefields, Wilmslow.

Nesbit, Rev. R. B., Easby Vicarage, Richmond.

Phillips, The Venerable Archdeacon, St. George's Vicarage, Barrow-in-Furness.
Powell, Rev. T. W., Old Croft, Stanwix, Carlisle.
Peile, Dr. John, Litt. D. Master of Christ's College, Cambridge.
Pease, E. T., Esq., Oak Lee, Darlington.
Petty, Lister, Esq., Bortree Stile, Ulverston.
Postlethwaite, G., Esq., Syle Croft, Millom.

Robinson, J., Esq., J.P., Westwood Hall, Leek, Staffordshire (6 copies).
Robinson, John, Esq., C.E., Vicarage Terrace, Kendal.

Stuart, Rev. J. C., Brunswick Chapel House, Leeds.
Smith, J. J., Esq., Abbey Town, Carlisle.
Simpson, Joseph, Esq., Romanway, Penrith.
Sewell, Colonel, Brandlingill, Cockermouth.
Sargeant, John Young, Esq., Sella Park, Carnforth (2 copies).
Savory, Sir J., Bart, M.P., Buckhurst Park, Ascot.
Smallpiece, Rev. John, St. Bees.

Thwaites, Thomas, Esq., C.C., Wood Lea, Kendal.
Thompson, W. N., Esq., St. Bees.
Thompson, Dr., M.D., Lightburne, Ulverston.
Tosh, E. G., Esq., The Lund, Ulverston.
Turner, Miss, 20, Cambridge Terrace, Hyde Park, London, W.

Vaughan, Cedric, Esq., J.P., Leyfield, Millom.

Warbrick, Mrs., Oreton Mount, Grange-over-Sands.
Walker, Rev. S. R. M., Seathwaite Vicarage, Broughton-in-Furness.
Whitwell, R. J., Esq., Florence.
Wilson, T. Esq., Aynam Lodge, Kendal.
Woodburne, Myles, Esq., Kirklands, Ulverston.
Wright, Dr. Hodgson, Park Road, Halifax (3 copies).
Wright, Rev. A., R.D., Vicar of Gilsland.

www.ingramcontent.com/pod-product-compliance
Lightning Source LLC
Chambersburg PA
CBHW032245080426

42735CB00008B/1006